PROJECT 2002

EFFECTIVE PROJECT MANAGEMENT IN EIGHT STEPS

PROJECT 2002

EFFECTIVE PROJECT MANAGEMENT IN EIGHT STEPS

Stephen L. Nelson

REDMOND
TECHNOLOGY
P R E S S

Project 2002:
Effective Project Management in Eight Steps

Copyright © 2002 Stephen L. Nelson

All rights reserved. No part of this book may be reproduced in any form or by any method or any means without the prior written permission of the publisher.

Published by
Redmond Technology Press
8581 154th Avenue NE
Redmond, WA 98052
www.redtechpress.com

Library of Congress Catalog Card No: Applied for

ISBN 1-931150-44-3

Printed and bound in the United States of America.

9 8 7 6 5 4 3 2 1

Distributed by
Independent Publishers Group
814 N. Franklin St.
Chicago, IL 60610
www.ipgbook.com

Product and company names mentioned herein may be the trademarks of their respective owners.

In the preparation of this book, both the author and the publisher have made every effort to provide current, correct, and comprehensible information. Nevertheless, inadvertent errors can occur and software and the principles and regulations concerning business often change. Furthermore, the application and impact of principles, rules, and laws can vary widely from case to case because of the unique facts involved. For these reasons, the author and publisher specifically disclaim any liability or loss that is incurred as a consequence of the use and application, directly or indirectly, of any information presented in this book. If legal or other expert assistance is needed, the services of a professional should be sought.

CONTENTS AT A GLANCE

	Introduction	xv
Step 1	**Learn the Language**	**1**
Step 2	**Describe the Project**	**23**
Step 3	**Schedule Project Tasks**	**39**
Step 4	**Identify and Allocate Resources**	**59**
Step 5	**Review Project Organization**	**89**
Step 6	**Present Project to Stakeholders**	**137**
Step 7	**Manage Project Progress**	**177**
Step 8	**Communicate Project Status**	**201**
Appendix A	**Deal with Project Complexity**	**213**
Appendix B	**Work with Multiple Projects**	**223**

Appendix C	**Customize Project**	**229**
	Glossary	**253**
	Index	**261**

CONTENTS

Introduction xv
    What Is Project 2002? xvi
    When Should You Use Project 2002? xvi
    A Note about Project 2002 and Project 2000 xvii
    What's in This Book? xviii
        Step 1: Learn the Language xviii
        Step 2: Describe the Project xviii
        Step 3: Schedule Project Tasks xviii
        Step 4: Identify and Allocate Resources xviii
        Step 5: Review Project Organization xix
        Step 6: Present Project to Stakeholders xix
        Step 7: Manage Project Progress xix
        Step 8: Communicate Project Status xix
        Appendix A: Deal with Project Complexity xix
        Appendix B: Work with Multiple Projects xix
        Appendix C: Customize Project xix
    Getting the Example Project Files xx
    Conventions Used in This Book xx

Step 1	**Learn the Language** 1
	What Is a Project? 2
	Understanding the Basics of Project Management 2
	1. Organizing the Pieces that Make Up the Project 3
	2. Establishing the Timing of the Tasks 5
	3. Identifying and Allocating Project Resources 10
	4. Monitoring Project Time, Resources, and Costs 12
	How Project 2002 Helps with Project Management 14
	Using Project to Organize and Show the Pieces of a Project 14
	Using Project to Show the Timing of Tasks 16
	Using Project to Manage Resources 18
	Using Project to Monitor Projects 21
	Summary 22
Step 2	**Describe the Project** 23
	Creating a Project File 23
	Choosing Where and How to Save Project Files 25
	Opening Project Files 27
	Using File Properties 28
	Setting Project Start and Finish Dates 29
	Setting Up a Project Calendar 30
	Making the Project Screen Work for You 36
	Summary 38
Step 3	**Schedule Project Tasks** 39
	Creating a To-Do List of Tasks and Durations 39
	Describing an Example Project 40

      Identifying and Scheduling Tasks 40
      Handling Tasks and Subtasks 43
      Recording Recurring Tasks 45
Fine-Tuning Duration Values 48
Identifying Task Dependencies 48
      Linking Tasks 49
      Removing Task Dependencies 50
      Handling Tasks that Overlap 51
      Adding Lag Time between Tasks 52
      Splitting Tasks 52
      Understanding the Types of Dependencies 52
Adding Other Scheduling Goals and Constraints 53
      Adding Milestones 54
      Adding Constraint Dates for Deadlines and Priority Tasks 55
      Resolving Dependency-Constraint Conflicts 56
Summary 58

Step 4 **Identify and Allocate Resources 59**

Allocating Resources 59
      Assigning Resources 60
      Specifying Parts and Equipment as Resources 61
      Removing Resources 63
      Substituting One Resource for Another 64
Fine-Tuning Duration Calculations for Resources 65
Creating Different Calendars for Groups of Resources 69
Editing Calendars for Individual Resources 71

  Reviewing Resource Allocations 74
    Using the Resource Sheet View 75
    Using the Resource Graph View 76
    Using the Resource Usage View 77
  Leveling Resources 78
    Leveling Resources Manually 78
    Leveling Resources Automatically 79
    Undoing Your Resource Leveling 82
  Assigning Costs to Resources 82
  Sharing Resources 84
    Setting Up a Resource Pool 85
    Using a Project File with a Shared Resource Pool 86
    Updating a Resource Pool 87
    Unlinking a Resource Pool 87
  Summary 88

Step 5   **Review Project Organization 89**

  Outlining Your Project 89
    Using Summary Tasks 90
    Using the Outlining Tools 91
    Editing or Deleting Summary Tasks 94
    Moving Tasks and Summary Tasks 96
    Collapsing and Expanding Tasks 97
    Adding Outline Symbols and Numbers 97
  Changing the Timescale 100
  Using Filters 102
    Standard Filters 103

Using Interactive Filters	113
Creating a Filter	114
Sorting Tasks and Resources	116
Looking at Your Project in Various Views	118
Understanding the Types of Views	119
The Views on the View Menu and View Bar	123
More Views	128
Displaying a Combination of Views	134
Creating a New View	135
Summary	136

Step 6 Present Project to Stakeholders 137

Printing Views of Your Project	138
Using Print Preview	138
Understanding the Page Setup Dialog Box	141
The Print Dialog Box	149
Generating Reports	151
Using the Reports Dialog Box	153
Understanding the Types of Reports	155
Customizing a Report	159
Creating a Report from an Existing Report	161
Exporting Project Information to Other Applications	163
Exporting to Excel	164
Exporting to Access	168
Exporting to HTML	168
Creating a New Export Map	170

Sending to Word 172

Copying Project Information to a Graphics File 174

Summary 176

Step 7 Manage Project Progress 177

Establishing and Using a Baseline 177

Setting the Baseline 178

Changing the Baseline 179

Updating Tasks 180

Updating the Schedule 182

Recording Actual Start and Finish Dates 182

Recording Actual Durations 184

Setting and Updating Costs 184

Estimating Task Costs 185

Reviewing Estimated Project Costs 186

Recording Actual Costs 188

Reviewing Actual Project Costs 191

Comparing Your Progress with Your Plan 192

Using the Tracking Gantt View 192

Using the Work Table 193

Using Progress Lines 195

Performing Earned Value Analysis 197

Viewing the Earned Value Tables 198

Viewing an Earned Value Report 199

Summary 200

Step 8	**Communicate Project Status**	**201**
	A Word about Microsoft Project Server and Project Central	202
	Declaring How You Want to Collaborate	202
	Getting Ready to Collaborate by E-Mail	203
	Recording Your Collaborators' E-Mail Addresses	204
	Assigning Tasks or Projects by E-Mail	206
	Updating Task Assignments	209
	Requesting Progress Information about a Task	209
	Sending a Project File	210
	Routing a File to Others	211
	Summary	212
Appendix A	**Deal with Project Complexity**	**213**
	Simplifying Dependency Relationships	213
	Dividing a Large Project into Multiple Subprojects	215
	Using WBS Codes	216
	Using Macros to Automate Actions	219
Appendix B	**Work with Multiple Projects**	**223**
	Creating a Consolidated Project File for Multiple Projects	223
	Updating Links of Source Projects	226
	Linking Tasks Across Separate Project Files	227
Appendix C	**Customize Project**	**229**
	Customizing Toolbars	229
	Adding and Deleting Buttons	230
	Changing Button Images	232

Creating a New Toolbar	234
Customizing Menus	236
Adding New Commands	237
Adding New Menus	238
Customizing a Table	239
Changing an Existing Table	239
Creating a New Table	242
Customizing the Gantt Chart	244
Changing the Display of Nonworking Time	245
Changing the Appearance of Bars	248
Changing the Appearance of All Bars	249
Adding Gridlines to the Chart	249
Changing the Default View	251

Glossary 253

Index 261

INTRODUCTION

On project managers' office walls, you sometimes see a poster that lists the following five stages in the life cycle of a project:

- Enthusiasm for the goal
- Disillusionment with the progress
- Search for the guilty
- Persecution of the innocent
- Praise for the nonparticipants

As a friend of mine is fond of saying, "It's like a joke, but it's not funny." Unfortunately, we've all managed projects in the past that could be summarized in these words.

If you've picked up this book in the bookstore or if you've just bought this book, you probably have a good reason for doing so. Maybe you've finished managing the project from hell, and you're sure there's a better way. Or maybe you're about to embark on a new project, and your enthusiasm has led you to consider setting it up in Microsoft Project 2002. You might also have used previous versions of Project, and you want your project management tools to be up-to-date.

Whatever the reason, if you're a busy executive, if you manage projects (large and complicated or small and compact), and if plowing through a thousand pages of technical jargon sounds more painful than a root canal, this book is for you. In a nutshell, I walk you through the eight steps of project management using Project 2002. Within each step, I summarize, describe, and list the actions you need to take to set up and record information about your project. I don't tell you everything there is to know about Project, because you don't need an encyclopedic knowledge of the program to manage your projects effectively.

Before getting into the details of what you will find in this book, I want to alert you to one of the pitfalls of using project management software. A few years ago, I had a department manager who had become completely enamored with a new project management application. The walls of his office were covered with PERT charts he had printed out along with other charts and diagrams. In essence, this guy spent more time managing his project management program than he did managing his projects. Project 2002 is a tool, not a deliverable. Its purpose is to make your life easier, not to complicate it. And as you'll soon see, this is my approach to using it.

You should also know that I've made some assumptions about you as I wrote this book. First, I assume that you are a knowledgeable and informed executive who has some experience using Microsoft Windows and Windows applications. You know how to use the mouse and how to select menu commands and access tools on a toolbar. Second, you're on speaking terms with the aspects of project management, and third, you're acquainted with the accounting practices that are typically involved in project management. That said, however, I also assume that from time to time you may need some detail, and I've included that where appropriate.

What Is Project 2002?

Microsoft Project 2002 is the latest version of a project management application that has been around since the mid-1980s. You can use it to plan and track the progress of a project using standard approaches to defining projects and organizing the tasks that make up a project, including Gantt charts, PERT charts, and variations on these themes. You can establish a baseline and then track how reality compares with it. You can allocate and monitor people and equipment, and you can track costs and compare them with your budget.

In addition, if you have access to a local area network, an intranet, or the Internet, you can use Project tools to communicate with others, post portions of your project on the Web, and send Project files as e-mail attachments.

When Should You Use Project 2002?

Project 2002 provides most of the tools and techniques you need to manage projects, whether you manage projects with hundreds or thousands of tasks and as many resources or you merely tap into Project's features and functions to think more clearly about organizing simple yet important projects. Regardless of where you fall in this spectrum, you will find that Project delivers five general benefits:

- Using Project lets you answer the question "What is a project?"

    This might seem obvious, but if you've managed any projects at all, you know that clarifying the use of a resource or assigning a task can become complicated if the project itself is not defined well. Using Project helps you answer this fundamental question.

- Using Project lets you answer the question "How will the project be accomplished?"

    If you see your project as one gigantic to-do list of random and disconnected tasks, you're going to be overwhelmed and so is anybody involved in the project. Using Project to organize your to-do list into tasks and subtasks and to identify what depends on what lets you see light at the end of the tunnel.

- Using Project lets you answer the question "When will the project and the parts of the project be completed?"

    Scheduling is essential when managing a project. You need to know when tasks will start and finish so that you can allocate human and equipment resources or perhaps even hire people with special skills. And, unless you have an unlimited amount of time and an unlimited budget (that is, you work in fantasyland), your organization will hold you responsible for the eventual outcome of your project and its completion date. Using Project, you can see at a glance where you are on the schedule and what needs to be done.

- Using Project lets you answer the question "Who or what will do the work?"

    You may need to answer only the preceding three questions, but if careful management of resources is key to the success of your project, you need Project. With Project's resource management features you can ensure that people and equipment are available on time and within budget.

- Using Project lets you answer the question "How is my project progressing compared with my plan?"

    When you set up a project in Project, you also establish a baseline plan that you (and Project) use to see how reality is stacking up against the schedule and the costs. Again, unless you work in fantasyland, this is an important issue.

A Note about Project 2002 and Project 2000

Although this book covers Project 2002, much of the instructions you will find here also apply to Project 2000, the earlier version of Project. If you have Project 2000 and you are considering this book, I encourage you to read this book as a guide to your Project 2000 software. The program changed here and there between 2000 and 2002, but it didn't change that much. The main difference between the two versions of the program has to do with the interface. The latest version of Project includes the Project Guide task pane, a way to complete tasks by using wizards instead of menu commands. Other than that, the two programs aren't so very different. That is, they aren't so very different that a savvy person couldn't employ this book as a guide to Project 2000.

What's in This Book?

As I mentioned earlier, this book is organized according to eight steps of project management. In addition to these steps, I've included three appendixes. Here's a rundown of what you'll find in each step and each appendix.

Step 1: Learn the Language

If you're new to project management, if it's been a long time since you took Project Management 101, or if you need to brush up on some terminology, make reading Step 1 your first step. It's really a project management primer that summarizes the process and then shows you how the process relates to Project 2002.

Step 2: Describe the Project

In this step, you create a project file, save it, resave it, open it again, and set up date parameters and a calendar for your project.

Step 3: Schedule Project Tasks

Here's where you take the to-do list out of your head and commit it to bits and bytes. As you begin to set up an example project, you identify and schedule tasks, specify durations (how long each task will take), insert dependencies (specify which tasks depend on others), add milestones and constraints, and resolve any constraint conflicts.

Step 4: Identify and Allocate Resources

Now it's time to allocate resources (both people and equipment), fine-tune durations, create calendars, review resource allocations, level resources as necessary, assign costs to resources, and share resources if necessary.

Step 5: Review Project Organization

As your plan shapes up, you can use Project to focus on it in various ways to verify that it will work. First, you can display it in outline form, a time-honored technique for imposing organization. You can then change the timescale, and you can filter your project information to display only certain aspects, such as people, tasks, or costs. You can also sort items and display your project in various views.

Step 6: Present Project to Stakeholders

A stakeholder is anyone who is involved or affected by your project. In this step, you print views of your project, generate and print reports about your project, and take a look at how to send your project file to other applications, including Microsoft Excel, Access, and Word.

Step 7: Manage Project Progress

With your project plan in place, you're now ready to start tracking its progress. In this step, you establish a baseline, record completed tasks, update the schedule, set and record costs, compare your progress with your plan, and perform earned value analysis.

Step 8: Communicate Project Status

In this step, you use the tools that Project provides to collaborate with others via e-mail on a project.

Appendix A: Deal with Project Complexity

This appendix explains the tacks you can take when projects become complex. It describes how to simplify dependency relationships, break a large project into smaller projects, use WBS codes to organize projects, and record macros to automate repetitive tasks.

Appendix B: Work with Multiple Projects

If you're like me, you're seldom working with only one project. This appendix shows you how to manage multiple projects with Project.

Appendix C: Customize Project

Project has a slick and easy-to-use interface, but you can change this interface to suit the way you work or prefer to work. This appendix describes how to customize toolbars, menus, column width, and more.

Getting the Example Project Files

Most of the project files you see in the figures of this book are available at the Redmond Technology Press Web site. If you want to see how a project looks on your screen or follow along at your computer, you can retrieve these files at *http://www.redtechpress.com/projects.zip*. The project files are compressed using the Windows XP zip format, so you need to unzip the projects.zip file before you can begin working with the files. In general, project files use the figure label as the filename.

Conventions Used in This Book

To distinguish between Microsoft Project 2002 and your project, I use the word *Project* (with an uppercase P) to refer to Microsoft Project the program. I use the word *project* (with a lowercase p) to refer to your project: the building you're constructing, the information system you're developing, or the marketing campaign you're running.

To identify screen elements, I capitalize the first letter of each word in the description. This convention looks a bit funny at first, but it makes it more likely that you'll understand some instruction such as "click the Cancel—Avoid The Scheduling Conflict button."

You'll also find Notes, Tips, and Warnings, which point out small tidbits of useful information. Pay attention to Warnings; they help you avoid potential problems.

Step 1

LEARN THE LANGUAGE

In This Step
- What is a project?
- What is project management?
- How does Project 2002 help?

If you're new to project management, the subject might confuse you at first. You have to learn a few new terms, make behind-the-scenes calculations, and master the complexities of the project you want to manage better.

To understand project management and effectively manage projects, you need to strip away the clutter, learn the language, and review the logic. Step 1 will help you prepare to manage projects by delving into these three questions:

1. What is a project?

2. What is project management?

3. How does Microsoft Project 2002 help?

When you finish with this Step, you should be able to determine whether you really want to use Project 2002 for a particular project and, if so, how you want to use Project 2002.

What Is a Project?

Because people have different conceptions of a "project," it makes sense to start off with a common definition. A *project* is an activity that has a defined start and a defined finish, produces some measurable result, and requires time, money, and resources to complete. Although that definition amounts to a rather abstract description, usually projects are concrete and easy to identify. For example, building a skyscraper, landscaping a parking lot, throwing a party, and making a movie are all projects. Each has a defined start and a defined finish. Each produces some measurable result. Each requires time, money, and resources.

Understanding the Basics of Project Management

Although the term *management* often refers to loosely defined qualitative activities, the term *project management* actually refers to a specific set of activities that pertain to making sure that a project is completed successfully. Project management encompasses these four activities:

1. Organizing and showing the individual pieces that make up the project.

2. Establishing the timing of tasks. Timing refers to the time required to complete tasks and when tasks start and stop.

3. Identifying and allocating the resources that are needed to complete the project.

4. Comparing the planned outcome with the actual outcome. Comparisons are usually made in three areas: time spent, resources required, and money spent.

Throughout this book, we will look at a sample project that involves the writing, editing, and publishing of a book. For now, however, consider what is required to complete a closer-to-home project: painting the interior of an apartment. The following pages explain the four basic principles of project management.

> **NOTE** *I chose a simple project on purpose. Painting an apartment makes it easy for you to concentrate on project management issues. Before you can use Project effectively, you need to know the basics of project management.*

1. Organizing the Pieces that Make Up the Project

Even in the case of a small project like painting the interior of an apartment, you benefit greatly by breaking the project into pieces and noting the relationships among the pieces. You might, for example, list six steps for the painting project:

1. Wash the walls you will paint.

2. Plug any holes with patching compound.

3. Tape window and door frames to protect them.

4. Buy the paint and brushes you need.

5. Paint the walls.

6. Clean up after you finish.

Each of these steps is called a *task*. In any project, you can perform some tasks at the same time. For example, the first four tasks—washing, plugging, taping, and buying—can occur in any order. If someone helps, these tasks can even occur at the same time.

In most projects, however, you need to complete some tasks before you can begin others. For example, you need to complete the first four tasks before you can start painting. And you should finish painting before you start the final task, cleaning up. The relationships between the various tasks are called *dependencies* because one task depends on another. These relationships are also called *links* because the start of one task is linked to the finish of another task. When one task depends on another, the task that you must finish first is called the *predecessor*. The task that must follow the predecessor is called the *successor*.

> **NOTE** *The Glossary at the end of this book explains terms such as* task, dependency, predecessor, *and* successor. *If you have any questions about a term, you can always turn to the Glossary.*

Some tasks consist of still smaller tasks or pieces. When a task is made up of multiple parts, these parts are called *subtasks*. For example, you can divide the cleaning-up task into four subtasks:

1. Locate any paint spills and remove them.

2. Clean the paintbrushes.

3. Remove the tape from around the windows and doorframes.

4. Put away the remaining paint and brushes.

One way to organize the pieces of a project is to create a list of tasks and subtasks, as I've just done on the preceding page. You can organize a project in other ways, too.

For example, you can organize project information with a PERT chart, as illustrated in the drawing in Figure 1-1. Figure 1-1 graphically depicts the six main tasks you need to complete for the imaginary painting project.

Figure 1-1   An example PERT chart.

PERT stands for *Program Evaluation and Review Technique.* A PERT chart shows a project's tasks and the task dependencies. A PERT chart also shows the relationships among tasks. In Figure 1-1, for example, the lines connecting the boxes show the order in which the tasks must be performed.

Listing project tasks and viewing a PERT chart can make a project easier to organize and manage. One big benefit, of course, is that you remember what you need to do to complete the project.

Another benefit of PERT charts is being able to visually organize and inspect the relationships among tasks. After reviewing Figure 1-1, for example, you may decide that other dependencies or links exist. Certainly, a PERT chart makes reviewing task dependencies easier.

Task lists and PERT charts become more important when you manage projects that involve a great number of tasks. Inadvertently missing a task or dependency is easier when a project encompasses numerous tasks. In a large project, you have to tap the skills of more people. If you manage a project with several dozen, several hundred, or several thousand people, achieving project success requires that everyone knows what the project entails and the order in which tasks should be completed. Task lists and PERT charts can help immensely.

2. Establishing the Timing of the Tasks

After deciding which tasks make up a project and how the tasks link, the next project-management issue is the timing of tasks. The timing of tasks consists of two parts: figuring out how much time a task takes and figuring out when a task starts and finishes.

Estimating Task and Project Durations

To show the timing of tasks, you first estimate the amount of time that each task will take. Suppose that you decide to organize the painting project, using the six main tasks. You might make the following estimates:

Washing—3 hours

Plugging—1 hour

Taping—1 hour

Buying—.5 hour

Painting—4 hours

Cleaning—.5 hour

The time taken to complete a task is called its *duration*. For example, the duration of the washing task equals 3 hours, and the duration of the plugging task equals 1 hour.

Some pieces of a project aren't really tasks at all, because their duration equals zero. When the duration of a piece equals zero, the piece is called a *milestone*. Typically, milestones represent events that don't require work but are significant landmarks in the project's schedule or life. For example, the Start and End boxes in Figure 1-1 represent milestones.

After you estimate task durations, you can determine how long the project will take to finish by identifying the *paths* through a project on a PERT chart. To move from the start of the project to the end of the project, you must follow a path. For example, the first path is to start the project with the Washing task, move to the Painting task, and then move to the Cleaning task.

Figure 1-1, in fact, shows four paths, or routes, through the PERT chart:

Path 1: Washing—Painting—Cleaning

Path 2: Plugging—Painting—Cleaning

Path 3: Taping—Painting—Cleaning

Path 4: Buying—Painting—Cleaning

If the term *path* seems confusing, place your finger on the Start box in Figure 1-1 and trace the lines that connect the Start box to the Washing box, the Washing box to the Painting box, the Painting box to the Cleaning box, and the Cleaning box to the End box. What you are tracing with your finger is the first of the four paths.

Each path has a duration that equals the total of the individual task durations making up the path. You can calculate path durations of the four tasks as follows:

Duration of path 1:

Washing: 3.0 hours

Painting: 4.0 hours

Cleaning   0.5 hour

Total: 7.5 hours

Duration of path 2:

Plugging: 1.0 hour

Painting: 4.0 hours

Cleaning   0.5 hour

Total: 5.5 hours

Duration of path 3:

Taping: 1.0 hour

Painting: 4.0 hours

Cleaning   0.5 hour

Total: 5.5 hours

Duration of path 4:

Buying: 0.5 hour

Painting: 4.0 hours

Cleaning   0.5 hour

Total: 5.0 hours

When you know the durations of each of the paths through the project, you know how long the project will take to finish in its entirety. Assuming at least one other person is helping you with the first four tasks of the painting project, you can estimate the project duration by identifying the *critical path*. The critical path is the series of tasks that must be completed on time in order for a project to finish on schedule. In the case of the four paths through the painting project, the critical path is the first one, Washing—Painting—Cleaning, which takes 7.5 hours. The project duration, then, equals 7.5 hours. This assumes that other people can do the taping, plugging, and paint purchasing for you.

NOTE *The 7.5-hour duration along the critical path assumes that you paint and clean alone. If someone helps with the painting and cleaning, you can shorten the task durations. Likewise, the project duration can only be as reasonable as the task durations you enter. So the project can also last much longer, especially if you take the unexpected into account. For example, if your dog knocks over a paint can and tracks paint throughout the apartment, the Cleaning task will take several times longer than you expected.*

Project-management systems like Project 2002 calculate the durations of each path through a project, identify the critical path, and give the project duration. In the simple painting project, making the required calculations doesn't require much work. But when projects include hundreds of tasks and dozens of paths, Project 2002 can help you map out projects, determine how long they will take to complete, and assign tasks.

At this point, you may be asking yourself why you would want to go to the effort of estimating durations so you can calculate the critical path. You will usually want to know your project's critical path for three reasons:

- Because the duration of the critical path equals the duration of the project, identifying the critical path lets you estimate when you will finish the project. In the case of the painting project, because the critical path equals 7.5 hours, you know that once you start the project, it will take at least 7.5 hours to complete.

- If you know which tasks are on the critical path, you know which tasks cannot be delayed without delaying the project. For example, the Painting task is on the critical path. If painting takes longer than 4 hours, your project takes longer than 7.5 hours.

- If you know which tasks aren't on the critical path, you know which tasks can be delayed without delaying the project. For example, the Buying task isn't on the critical path. So, to some extent, the Buying task can be delayed without delaying the project. The amount of time a task can be delayed without delaying the project is called *slack*. To determine the actual amount of slack, you need to know when a task can start and when a task must finish, which is the subject of the next section.

Using Start and Finish Dates and Times

After figuring out how much time a task takes, the next consideration is the start and finish date of each task. You can calculate four dates and times for each task:

- Early start: The earliest date or time you can begin work on a task.
- Early finish: The earliest date or time you can expect to complete a task.
- Late start: The latest date or time you can begin work on a task without delaying the project.
- Late finish: The latest date or time you can complete a task without delaying the project.

Does knowing when tasks need to be initiated and completed help? Yes, especially if a project involves a large number of tasks.

Calculating start and finish dates and times isn't difficult, but the arithmetic can be rather tedious. Thankfully, Project 2002 performs the arithmetic for you. To calculate the start and finish dates of tasks in a project, you provide early and late start and finish dates, and Project 2002 makes the time calculations. The process goes something like this:

1. **Identify when you will start the project.**

   Suppose that in the painting example, you decide you will start next Saturday at 8 A.M. The project start time, then, equals 8 A.M.

2. **Calculate the finish time of the project.**

   Project 2002 makes this calculation by adding the durations of all the tasks in the critical path. For example, in the case of the painting project, you begin with the project start time of 8 A.M. and then add the 3 hours of washing, the 4 hours of painting, and the 0.5 hour of cleaning. This formula gives you the finish time, 3:30 P.M.

3. **Calculate the early start of each task.**

   Starting with the first task in each path, the early start of each task in the path is calculated by adding the duration of the predecessor task to the early start time of the predecessor task. For the first task in a path, because there is no predecessor task, the start of the project is used in the calculation.

4. **Calculate the early finish of each task.**

   To calculate the early finish of each task, the duration of the task is added to the early start of the task. For example, to calculate the early finish of the Washing task, the early start of the Washing task (8 A.M.) is added to the duration of the Washing task (3 hours). The early finish of the Washing task equals 11 A.M.

   In this example, the latest of the early starts is 11 A.M., which is when the Washing task finishes. Because you cannot start painting until you finish washing, picking the latest of the early start dates means you're sure that you have completed the predecessor tasks that finish last.

5. **Calculate the late finish of each of the paths.**

   Starting with the last task in each of the paths, the late finish of each task in each path is calculated by subtracting the duration of the successor task from the late finish of the successor task. For the last task in a path, because there is no successor path, the project finish is used.

   The late finishes of tasks in each of the remaining paths is calculated in a similar fashion. As with calculating the early starts, however, there is a twist: When a task appears on more than one path, you end up calculating several late finishes.

6. **Calculate the late start of each task.**

   The late start of each task is calculated by subtracting the duration of the task from its late finish. For example, to calculate the late start of the Buying task, subtract the Buying task duration, 0.5 hour, from the late finish of the Buying task.

7. **Calculate task slack.**

   To determine task slack, calculate the difference between the early and late start or the difference between the early and late finish. Either calculation produces the same result because the task duration determines the difference between the early start and finish and between the late start and finish. The difference equals the amount of slack in a task—the amount that a task start or finish can be delayed without delaying the project.

3. Identifying and Allocating Project Resources

The third aspect of project management is identifying and allocating the resources you require to complete a project. Typically, you need people and equipment to complete tasks. And because resources are limited, you usually need to organize your projects with an eye to available resources.

Take, again, the example project of painting an apartment. If you add the durations of all the tasks, the project in total requires 10 hours of time from one or more persons. That's a resource. If you're painting the ceilings, the project probably requires ladders or step stools. Those are resources, too. In any project, you want to make sure that your plans identify and schedule use of resources.

Here are the general actions you take to recognize the resources you need for a project:

1. List the resources that are available to you.

2. Allocate resources to project tasks.

3. Adjust for discrepancies between the resources that are available and the resources you need.

In listing the available resources, include both people and equipment. For the painting project, for example, people resources include yourself and perhaps a helpful friend. Your equipment resources include a ladder, paintbrushes, a paint roller and pan, and drop cloths to protect your furniture and carpet from paint. You can actually create a resources list from this information:

Me

My best friend

A 10-foot ladder

Two paintbrushes

A paint roller and pan

Two 10-by-16-foot drop cloths

In allocating resources, you commit a resource to a task and, as a result, take the resource off the list of available resources for the time that you've scheduled it. While your best friend is allocated to the task of washing the walls, for example, his or her name is removed from the resources list. If you allocate the use of the ladder for plugging holes with patching compound, the ladder is removed from the resources list.

After you complete the first two steps of recognizing project resources, you need to resolve any discrepancies between what the project needs and what is actually available to allocate. Essentially, you verify that neither of the following error conditions exists:

1. Resource shortages

2. Resource overallocations

A *resource shortage* is a situation in which you need a resource to complete a task, but the resource is not available. For example, if the painting project calls for you, a single individual, to complete the job within the 7.5-hour project duration, you need more than one person if the project amounts to 10 hours of work.

A *resource overallocation* is a situation in which you allocate a resource to different tasks and these tasks require the same resource at the same time. If your painting project calls for the ladder to be used simultaneously—by you as you plug holes and by your best friend when he or she washes the walls—a resource overallocation exists.

> **NOTE** *A resource overallocation also occurs when a task requires more time than a resource can provide. For example, if a person works 8 hours a day but a task requires 16 hours a day of work, the person is overallocated.*

The process of rescheduling a project's tasks so that resource overallocations are eliminated is called *resource leveling*. Resource leveling generally involves stretching out the work on tasks so that resources are used more evenly. Resource leveling can also stretch out the critical path and make the project take longer to complete.

In the painting project, for example, the project's critical path is 7.5 hours and the project requires 10 hours of work. If you can't get a friend's help and therefore end up doing all 10 hours of work yourself, you won't be able to finish the 10-hour project in a mere 7.5 hours. You'll be overallocated. Assuming you can't recruit another friend, your only recourse is to stretch out the 10 hours of work over 10 or more hours. In this case, you are practicing resource leveling.

With only a handful of tasks and a short list of resources, identifying and allocating resources might not be worth the effort. Most projects, however, benefit from resource allocation and leveling. Even in relatively small projects, forgetting about a resource or inadvertently overallocating a resource is a simple mistake that many people make. Project 2002 eliminates those mistakes.

4. Monitoring Project Time, Resources, and Costs

The fourth component of project management consists of monitoring the actual time spent on tasks, the actual resources that are used to complete tasks, and the actual cost of a project. Traditionally, you monitor these three characteristics—time, resources, and cost—by comparing what you planned with what actually occurs.

Sometimes this business of comparing planned figures with actual figures gives you unfavorable results. Unfortunately, the comparisons often show that a project is progressing more slowly, is using more resources, and is costing more money than you originally planned. However, the comparisons provide you with an early warning system. And, often, the early warnings give you time to remedy problems when they are little rather than big.

A common technique for monitoring project time, resources, and costs is *earned value analysis*. Earned value analysis refers to the very logical process of comparing the planned progress and cost of a task with the actual progress and cost.

Take the Painting task in the example apartment-painting project. If the project schedule indicates that the task will take 4 hours, starting at 11 A.M. and finishing at 3 P.M., you can use this information to manage the completion of the task. To do so, you compare the planned work with the actual work to see whether work is progressing at the planned rate. For example, you could verify that painting begins at 11 A.M. and verify at periodic intervals that work continues at the planned rate. You could verify at 12 P.M., 1 hour into the planned painting task, that someone has actually been painting for an hour. You could verify at 1 P.M., 2 hours into the painting project, that someone has actually been painting for 2 hours, and so on.

> **NOTE** *Comparing planned work with actual work might be done on the basis of hours, as illustrated in the preceding paragraph, but these kinds of comparisons can also be performed using cost. In the case of the painting project, if you were paying your friend $10 an hour, you could also check to see that you had incurred $10 of painting cost after painting one wall, $20 after painting two walls, and so on.*

Comparing planned work with actual work is often very useful for assessing whether resources are being used according to a schedule or plan. Unfortunately, however, the comparison doesn't indicate whether the original duration estimates are reasonable. Nevertheless, you can often make another comparison that lets you assess the goodness of your duration estimates: You can compare the planned work scheduled in a certain interval to planned work performed in the same interval.

For the sake of simplicity, suppose in the imaginary painting project that you will paint four walls but not the ceiling. Further suppose that all four walls are roughly the same amount of work and will be painted by a friend paid $10 an hour. In this case, you could also say, because the task duration is estimated as 4 hours, that your plan is to paint one wall each hour at a cost of $10 a wall. At 12 P.M., 1 hour into the Painting task, you could verify not only whether someone has been working for an hour but whether he or she has painted one of the four walls. If the person has been painting an hour but hasn't yet finished a wall, you would know that your original duration estimates were suspect.

NOTE *The key to making comparisons of actual work performed and planned work performed is to have some metric that quantifies the actual work.*

Figure 1-2 shows an earned value analysis graph that plots work scheduled and work performed. What the graph shows in this case is that initial progress is slow but catches up by the end.

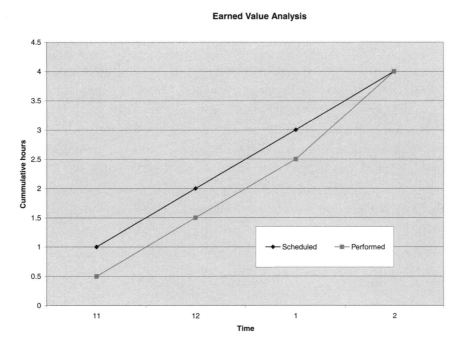

Figure 1-2 An earned value analysis graph compares cumulative work scheduled and cumulative work performed.

***Step 1** Learn the Language*

How Project 2002 Helps with Project Management

Project 2002 includes features that help with the four components of project management that were written up in the previous pages: organizing and showing the individual pieces that make up a project; establishing the timing of tasks; identifying and allocating the resources needed to complete a project; and comparing the planned outcome with the actual outcome in terms of time spent, resources required, and money spent.

Project 2002 gives you a collection of tools for creating project schedules. Using tools and numerous reports, you can view project information in different ways, analyze a project and track its progress, and communicate about the project with other people.

NOTE *Many tools, views, and reports perform two and sometimes even three of the four components of project management.*

Using Project to Organize and Show the Pieces of a Project

Project provides one view of a project that is particularly powerful for listing project tasks and visualizing and linking the tasks that make up the project: Gantt Chart view. Most of the time you work with Project, you'll probably use this view.

The Gantt Chart view includes two sections, as shown in Figure 1-3. The Gantt table on the left lists the pieces of the project and contains information about them, including the task names and durations. The Gantt chart on the right shows the tasks of the project as horizontal bars plotted against a time-scale, so you can see how long tasks take, when tasks start, and when tasks finish. Figure 1-3 shows a Gantt chart of the painting project. Slack in a Gantt chart shows up as a line. For example, the lines that trail from the Plug, Tape, and Buy task bars indicate that these tasks can be delayed a bit without delaying the start of the next successor task, Paint.

Figure 1-3   A Gantt chart.

NOTE *Project assumes people don't work over the lunch hour, which is why in Figure 1-3 the hour from 12:00 P.M. to 1:00 P.M. shows a dark shadow. In "Step 2: Describe the Project," I describe how to set up the project calendar, which is where Project gets information about when people work and don't work.*

Project also allows you to create PERT charts (it calls them Network Diagrams), as described earlier and illustrated in Figure 1-1. Network Diagrams provide an excellent format for assessing the tasks in a project and the order in which the tasks must be completed. Figure 1-4 shows most of a Network Diagram of the painting project.

Figure 1-4 A Network Diagram (or PERT chart).

In a Network Diagram, you can learn details about each task by looking in each task's box. You can learn the name of task, its duration and ID number, the date it begins and ends, its progress thus far and the resource that was assigned to it. Network Diagrams display milestones as rectangles, critical tasks as hexagons, and summary tasks as octagons.

Using Project to Show the Timing of Tasks

The Gantt Chart view, as described above, shows the timing of tasks, but to better see the to-do list for a certain period of time, you can switch to Calendar view, as shown in Figure 1-5.

Figure 1-5 The Calendar view.

By double-clicking a day, you can see the list of tasks scheduled for that day, as shown in Figure 1-6.

Figure 1-6 A to-do list for a day.

NOTE *To change the time span shown in the Calendar view, choose the View menu's Zoom command and select a different time span in the Zoom dialog box.*

Step 1 Learn the Language **17**

Using Project to Manage Resources

Project also provides tools and reports for managing project resources. To verify that you have remembered to allocate resources to each task in a project, you can view the Gantt chart. Look in the rightmost column of information in the table to see the assigned resource. The bars in the chart also name the resource, as shown in Figure 1-7. Obviously, tasks that don't show resources may need to be assigned resources.

Figure 1-7 A Gantt chart with an expanded task area so you can see assigned resources.

To verify that you haven't overallocated a resource, you can view a resource graph like the one in Figure 1-8. By comparing allocated resources with the actual resources that are available, you can ascertain whether you're planning to use more of a resource—a person or a piece of equipment—than is available.

18 *Project 2002: Effective Project Management in Eight Steps*

Figure 1-8 A resource graph.

NOTE *It's impossible to see in a black-and-white image like that shown in Figure 1-8, but red bars in resource graphs identify where overallocations have occurred.*

Another useful tool for more closely exploring why resource allocations exist is the Resource Sheet, as shown in Figure 1-9. A Resource Sheet lists resource allocations by task. The sheet totals individual task-level resource allocations so you can see what the total allocation is.

Figure 1-9   A Resource Sheet.

A Resource Sheet may not seem particularly useful in a simple project like the apartment painting example in this chapter, but it can be very useful in large projects with dozens of tasks and resources. In a large project, a Resource Sheet lets you easily see whether anyone is being overscheduled or underscheduled.

Another noteworthy resource-management feature of Project is its resource leveling tools. You can tell Project to stretch out the work on tasks where slack is available. When Project levels resources, it smoothes out and reschedules resource usage to avoid or at least minimize overallocation.

NOTE   *Resource leveling is described in "Step 4: Identify and Allocate Resources."*

Using Project to Monitor Projects

The fourth and final component of project management is monitoring project time, resources, and cost. Monitoring is done by comparing the work you scheduled with the work performed. With Project, you can get information about planned time, actual time, resources, and cost information. Monitoring these three factors is easy. Figure 1-10, for example, shows a Tracking Gantt view that compares actual progress with an original estimate.

Figure 1-10 A Tracking Gantt chart.

NOTE *Establishing a baseline and comparing it with actual progress is described in "Step 7: Manage Project Progress."*

Project shows each task using two bars. One bar shows planned work. One bar shows actual work. Project also adds completion percentages to the view. If a task is running behind, Project displays its bar in red.

Summary

This first Step gets you started by explaining the language and logic of project management. To accomplish this, the Step describes what a project is and identifies the four components of project management: organizing the pieces that make up a project; establishing the timing of project tasks; identifying and allocating project resources; and monitoring project time, resources, and cost. This Step also describes in general terms how you can use Project to help with each of these four tasks.

In "Step 2: Describe the Project," you begin reading about the process of describing a complex project to Project so you can use its tools to plan, organize, and monitor a project that involves the writing, editing, and publishing of a book.

Step 2

DESCRIBE THE PROJECT

Tasks Required to Complete the Step
- Creating a project file
- Setting project start and finish dates
- Setting up a project calendar

In order to use Microsoft Project, you must begin by describing the project in very general terms. This first step includes creating the Project file in which you will store all the project information.

Of course, to create a file, you must start Project first. Start Project in the same way that you start other Microsoft Windows programs. For example, click the Start button, choose Programs, and then click Microsoft Project. Project starts and opens a new, blank project.

Creating a Project File

Predictably, you store project information in a file. You can create a Project file after you've entered the information, but it makes more sense to create the file first. This way, you can easily save your changes as you work (and also have Project periodically save your changes automatically).

How you create a Project file depends on whether you are currently working on a file, you just started Project, or you want to use a wizard to create a file:

- Just started Project: A new, empty file with the generic name "Project1" is already open.

- Currently working on a file: Save the file you are working in and choose the File menu's New command, press Ctrl+N, or click the New toolbar button. You can also click the Blank Project link in the New Project task pane.

- Use a wizard: Click the Tasks button on the Project Guide toolbar and choose the first link, Define The Project. Then complete the four steps by entering information in the Project Guide task pane. You will be asked for a start date and whether you intend to collaborate with others.

> **TIP** *Project offers template files that you can use to get a jump-start on projects. Templates include Engineering, New Products, and New Business projects. To create a file from a template, start in the New Project task pane (if you don't see it, open the View menu, choose Toolbars, and choose Task Pane). Then, in the New Project task pane, click the General Templates hyperlink. The Templates dialog box opens. Click the Project Templates tab, select a template, and click OK.*

Save and name your file after you create it. To do so, choose the File menu's Save command, press Ctrl+S, or click the Save toolbar button. Project displays the Save As dialog box, as shown in Figure 2-1. Choose a folder location for the new file, enter a name for the file, and click the Save button.

Figure 2-1   The Save As dialog box.

TIP *If you want to create a new project file using the open project file, you can choose the File menu's Save As command and specify a new filename and location.*

Some people prefer to clamp a password on their Project files. If you are one of those people, choose the File menu's Save As command, click the Tools button in the Save As dialog box, and choose the General Options command. Project displays the Save Options dialog box, as shown in Figure 2-2. To prevent unauthorized access to the file, enter a password in the Protection Password box. To protect unauthorized modification of the file, enter a password in the Write Reservation Password box. If you want Project to prompt users to open the file as read-only, select the Read-Only Recommended check box. Next time you or someone else tries to enter the file, the Password dialog box appears.

Figure 2-2   The Save Options dialog box.

TIP *To remove a password from a Project file, choose the File menu's Save As command. Then, in the Save As dialog box, click the Tools button and choose General Options. You see the Save Options dialog box. Delete the password(s) and click OK. When you click the Save button in the Save As dialog box, Project asks if you want to replace the existing file. Click OK.*

Choosing Where and How to Save Project Files

Project offers a couple of options to make saving files a tad easier. If you're the type who is not very good about saving files, you can tell Project to save them automatically whenever a certain number of minutes has elapsed. And if you're the type who doesn't like rooting around in the Save As dialog box to find the folder where you keep your Project files, you can make your preferred folder's name appear in the dialog box right away.

Follow these actions to decide where and how to save Project files:

1. Choose the Tools menu's Options command.

Project displays the Options dialog box.

2. Click the Save tab.

The Save tab is shown in Figure 2-3.

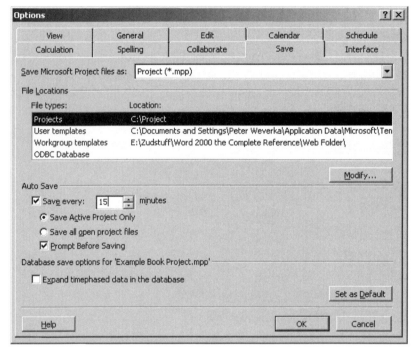

Figure 2-3 The Save tab of the Options dialog box.

3. Choose the folder where you want to save the majority of your files.

To do that, Make sure Projects is selected under File Types, and then click the Modify button. The Modify Location dialog box appears. It looks and works exactly like the Save As dialog box. Select the folder where you want to store Project files and click OK.

Back in the Options dialog box, the name of the folder you chose appears under File Types.

4. **Click the Save Every check box and enter a number in the Minutes box if you want to Project to save copies of your files.**

   Every number of minutes you specify, Project will display a dialog box so you can save your file. If you often work with more than one file, consider selecting the Save All Open Project Files option button as well.

5. **Click OK to close the Options dialog box.**

Opening Project Files

Project offers a bunch of different ways to open files:

- On the File menu: Names of the last four files you opened appear at the bottom of the File menu. Click a name to open a file.

- On the New Project task pane: Names of files you recently opened appear on the New Project task pane, as shown in Figure 2-4. (To view the task pane if it isn't open, choose the View menu's Toolbars command and choose Task Pane.) Under Open A Project, click the name of the file you want to open.

   TIP *You can make more than four filenames appear on the File menu or New Project task pane. Choose the Tools menu's Options command. Then, on the General tab of the Options dialog box, look for the Recently Used File List and enter a number higher than 4.*

- Click the Open toolbar button or press Ctrl+O. Then, in the Open dialog box shown in Figure 2-4, locate and select the file you want to open and double-click it or click the Open button.

Figure 2-4 Opening a Project file.

TIP *Project allows you to open more than one file at a time. Each file is displayed in its own document window. To move to another document window, choose the project file from the Window menu or select a button on the Windows taskbar.*

Using File Properties

Optionally, you can use the File menu's Properties command to collect or store additional miscellaneous information about a file. To use the File menu's Properties command in this manner, choose the command and click the Summary tab. Project displays the Properties dialog box, as shown in Figure 2-5. You can use the boxes provided to record such items as the author, company, and any comments.

Figure 2-5 The Summary tab of the Properties dialog box.

Setting Project Start and Finish Dates

After you've created the new project file, the next step is to identify either the project start or finish date as the date that you'll use to anchor the project schedule. It usually makes sense to anchor the project using a start date and then work from there. In this way, you implicitly build your schedule around the day you can start working.

However, you also anchor the project using a finish date, but that is a risky proposition because it doesn't really take into account effort that will go into completing the project. With this approach, you implicitly say that completing the project on time is more important than other project characteristics, including the cost of the project, realistic time estimates, and the quality of the deliverable.

> **WARNING** *In general, you shouldn't anchor a project to a finish date unless you're experienced in organizing and managing projects like the one you're describing.*

To identify the project start and finish dates, take the following actions:

1. Choose the Project menu's Project Information command.

Project displays the Project Information dialog box, as shown in Figure 2-6.

Figure 2-6 The Project Information dialog box.

2. **Choose an option in the Schedule From drop-down menu.**

   Very likely, you will choose Project Start Date, but if you want to anchor the project on the finish date, choose Project Finish Date.

3. **Set the start or finish date.**

   Click the Start Date or Finish Date box and enter a date. You can click the down arrow at the end of the Start Date box or Finish Date box to display a pop-up monthly calendar and use it to select a date.

4. **Click OK.**

   Project saves the start or finish date information and closes the Project Information dialog box.

Setting Up a Project Calendar

Project supplies a standard calendar, which identifies days and dates and some common nonworking days. But to complete your description of the project, you'll want to fine-tune this calendar so it reflects any local customs or company conventions about, for example, holidays.

> **NOTE** *The following pages describe how to set up a calendar the conventional way, but Project also offers a wizard for doing the job. If you are more comfortable working with wizards, click the Tasks button on the Project Guide toolbar and choose the Define General Working Times link on the Project Guide pane.*

To set up a project calendar that accurately describes the working dates available within the project start and finish dates, take the following actions:

1. **Choose the Tools menu's Change Working Time command.**

   Project displays the Change Working Time dialog box, as shown in Figure 2-7.

Figure 2-7   The Change Working Time dialog box.

2. **Indicate you want to create a new calendar.**

   Click the New button to tell Project you want to create a new calendar of working and nonworking time. Project displays the Create New Base Calendar dialog box, as shown in Figure 2-8.

Figure 2-8   The Create New Base Calendar dialog box.

3. **Name the new base calendar.**

   Enter the name you want to use for the project calendar.

   If the calendar's schedule of working and nonworking days will be specifically for the project, you might want to name it in a way that clearly identifies the connection to the project. A calendar for a plant relocation project might be named Plant Relocation Calendar.

If the calendar's schedule of working and nonworking days will work for other projects you or your company manages, you might want to name it in a way that clearly makes this distinction. A calendar for Acme Distributing might be named Standard Acme Calendar.

4. **Copy an existing schedule's information as a starting point.**

   Click the Make A Copy Of option button, select one of the existing calendars of working and nonworking time from the drop-down list box, and then click OK. Table 2-1 describes each of the three standard calendars you can copy to create a starting point for your own calendar.

CALENDAR	DEFAULT WORKING TIMES
Standard	8 A.M. to 5 P.M., five days a week
Night Shift	11 P.M. to 8 A.M., five days a week
24 Hours	12 A.M. to 12 A.M., seven days a week

Table 2-1   Descriptions of default project calendars you can copy.

5. **Describe the typical workweek and workday.**

   When Project redisplays the Change Working Time dialog box after you click OK at the end of the last action, click the Options button. When Project displays the Calendar tab of the Options dialog box, as shown in Figure 2-9, describe the typical workweek and workday:

   - Use the Week Starts On and Fiscal Year Starts In boxes to indicate when the workweek and work year begin.

   - Use the Default Start Time and Default End Time boxes to indicate when the workday typically starts and ends.

   - Use the Hours Per Day, Hours Per Week, and Days Per Month boxes to indicate how many hours are available in a day and week and how many days are available in a typical month.

   Click OK when you finish making these specifications to return to the Change Working Time dialog box.

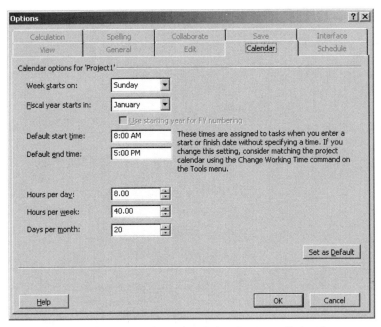

Figure 2-9 The Calendar tab of the Options dialog box.

NOTE *Project uses the Hours Per Day, Hours Per Week, and Days Per Month values to convert the task durations you enter from one time measurement to another time measurement. If you indicate a task will take one month, for example, Project assumes that's the same thing as twenty days if the Days Per Month value is set to 20. If you indicate a task will take one day, Project assumes that's the same thing as eight hours if the Hours Per Day value is set to 8.*

6. Identify project nonworking days.

To identify nonworking days, such as company holidays, use the calendar shown on the Change Working Time dialog box to show the month with the holidays. You can move backward or forward in the calendar by dragging the slider on the vertical scroll bar next to the calendar.

When the month you want shows, press and hold down the Ctrl key and click each of the days you want to mark as nonworking days.

After you've done this, click the Nonworking Time option button. Figure 2-10 shows July 3 through July 4, 2003, marked as nonworking days.

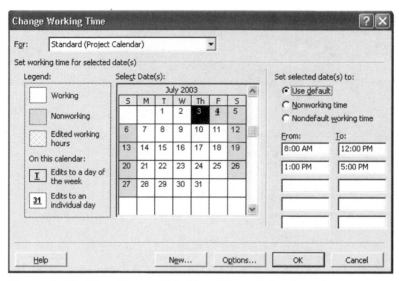

Figure 2-10 The Change Working Time dialog box showing nonworking days.

TIP *Different countries and localities often use different work calendars. If you're managing a project that includes people in Canada and Japan, for example, you won't be able to create a standard calendar that works for people in both locations. In this case, what you need to do is create a very general project calendar that doesn't identify unique cultural or country holidays. Instead, what you'll need to do is deal with these calendar issues at the resource calendar level. Resource calendars are described in "Step 4: Identify and Allocate Resources."*

7. **Describe exceptions to the typical workday or workweek.**

To identify any exceptions to the typical workday or workweek, use the calendar shown on the Change Working Time dialog box to show the month with the exceptions.

When the month you want shows, press and hold down the Ctrl key and click each of the days with the exception.

After you do this, click the Nondefault Working Time option button and use the From and To boxes to describe the exception. Figure 2-11 shows July 3, 2003, as just a four-hour workday, which is an exception to the typical eight-hour workday.

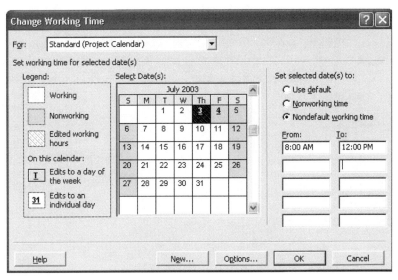

Figure 2-11 The Change Working Time dialog box—this time showing an exception to the usual eight-hour workday.

NOTE *The Change Working Time dialog box provides a legend explaining how working, nonworking, and nondefault working times appear on the calendar.*

8. Save your calendar changes.

Click OK to save your calendar changes. To save the project file with all your changes, click the Save toolbar button.

NOTE *When you're finished working in Project and have saved your changes, click the Close button in the upper right corner of the Microsoft Project window to close Project. If you've made changes to open projects and haven't saved these changes, Project prompts you to do so.*

If you want to make the calendar available for use in other projects, you need to also add the calendar to the global template. For example, if you followed the procedures above to create a company calendar, you would probably want to use this calendar in future projects. To add a calendar to the global Project template, take the following actions:

1. Choose the Tools menu's Organizer command.

Project displays the Organizer dialog box.

2. **Click the Calendars tab.**

   Figure 2-12 shows this tab. By default, the calendars available in the open Project file appear on the right and the calendars available in the global template appear on the left. The drop-down list boxes at the bottom of the dialog box specify which project or template is displayed.

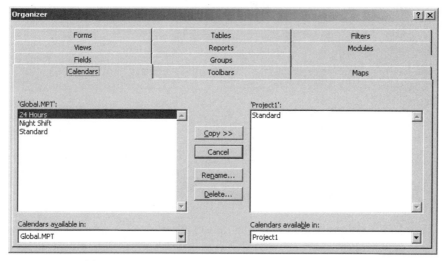

Figure 2-12 The Calendars tab of the Organizer dialog box.

3. **Select the calendar you want to copy to the global template, and click the <<Copy button.**

   Project adds the calendar to the list on the left.

4. **When you're finished, click the dialog box's Close button.**

   Click the small button with an X in the upper right corner of the dialog box to close the dialog box.

   TIP *To remove a calendar you've erroneously added or no longer need, display the Organizer dialog box, select the calendar you want to remove, and click the Remove button. Note that if you included the calendar in more than one template, you'll need to remove it from each template.*

Making the Project Screen Work for You

The Project screen can get pretty crowded. Whenever you change views (by choosing a command on the View menu), a new project guide appears in the Project Guide task pane on the left side of the screen. The screen offers numerous toolbars. Although this stuff is helpful, it sometimes gets in the way. Fortunately, you can do a lot to make the screen look the way you want it to look.

Here are some actions you can take to gain more real estate on the Project screen:

- Removing the Project Guide task pane: Click the task pane's Close button (the X) or click the Show/Hide Project toolbar button on the Project Guide toolbar.

- Permanently removing the Project Guide task pane: Choose the Tools menu's Options command, and then click the Interface tab of the Options dialog box, as shown in Figure 2-13. Uncheck the Display Project Guide check box and click OK.

- Removing the Project Guide toolbar: Choose the View menu's Toolbars command, and then unselect the Project Guide option on the submenu. You can also right-click any toolbar and uncheck Project Guide on the shortcut menu.

- Putting the Standard and Formatting toolbar on one row: You can save a little space by putting these toolbars on a single row. To do that, click the Toolbar Options button (the rightmost button on the Standard and the Formatting toolbar) and choose Show Buttons On One Row on the drop-down menu. To see two rows again, click the button a second time but choose Show Buttons On Two Rows.

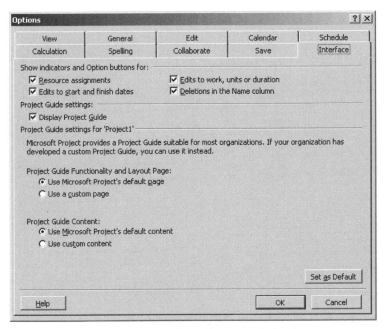

Figure 2-13 Interface tab of the Options dialog box.

Step 2 Describe the Project

TIP *Another way to change views is to do so with a wizard. Click the Report button on the Project Guide toolbar. Then, in the task pane, click the Select A View Or Report hyperlink and answer the questions to let Project choose which view is best for you.*

Summary

The first step you take to use Project 2002—the step of describing your project in general terms—isn't difficult. All you're doing, essentially, is describing the window of time into which your project needs to fit. But this important step lays a foundation for the next two steps you take, "Step 3: Schedule Project Tasks" and "Step 4: Identify and Allocate Resources."

Step 3

SCHEDULE PROJECT TASKS

Tasks Required to Complete the Step
- Creating a to-do list of tasks and durations
- Collecting additional task information
- Fine-tuning duration values
- Identifying task dependencies
- Adding other scheduling goals and constraints

After you complete "Step 2: Describe the Project," you can accurately describe and schedule the project's tasks. Fortunately, this step isn't much more difficult than creating a well-thought-out to-do list.

Creating a To-Do List of Tasks and Durations

While it's easy to let the work and complexity of a project overwhelm project team participants, you'll often find it quite straightforward to think about a project as a thorough to-do list.

> **NOTE** *If you just happen to have a to-do list in Microsoft Outlook that would serve as the starting point for creating tasks in Project, you can import your Outlook list into the Project file. To do so, choose the Tools menu's Import Outlook Tasks command. Then select the tasks you want to import and click OK.*

Describing an Example Project

For example, consider the project of publishing a document such as a book or report. At the highest level, you might say such a project consists of three tasks:

1. Write the book
2. Print the book
3. Sell the book

If these tasks were really groups of tasks requiring work from one or more than one person—as is typical—you might further expand this to-do list to a series of tasks and subtasks:

1. Write the book
    A. Research the book's content
    B. Create an outline
    C. Write the rough draft
    D. Edit the rough draft to create a final manuscript
2. Print the book
    A. Prepare the book for printing by desktop publishing
    B. Print the book
3. Sell the book
    A. Distribute the book to retailers
    B. Promote the book to potential readers

In actuality, some of the subtasks listed here could be broken down even further into sub-subtasks. In any event, the starting point for using Microsoft Project 2002 to schedule tasks is to record the project's to-do list.

Identifying and Scheduling Tasks

Once you know what tasks are required to complete a project—often this information is in your head—you're ready to identify and schedule these tasks. To identify and schedule tasks, take the following actions:

1. **Click the first empty row in the Task Name column and enter a task description.**

   Figure 3-1 shows how the first empty row of the Task Name column looks after it has been clicked and a task description has been entered. If you don't see the Task Name column, choose the View menu's Gantt Chart command.

   When you finish your entry, press the Tab key, press the right arrow key, or click the first empty row in the duration box.

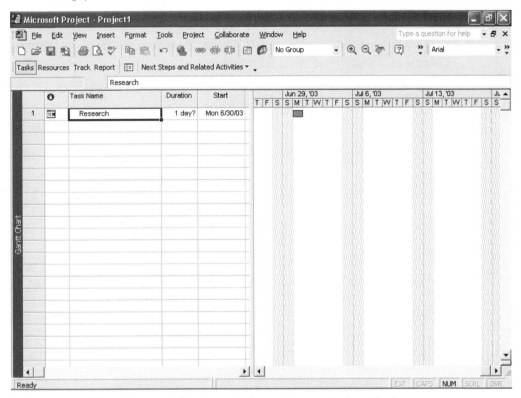

Figure 3-1 The Microsoft Project window with a task described.

TIP *You can make more room for task information by dragging the bar that separates the task information area from the Gantt chart area. Likewise, to make the Task Name column wider, thereby allowing more room for descriptive task names, drag the right edge of the Task Name column heading. You can also double-click the right edge of the Task Name column heading to size the column just wide enough to hold the longest task name. If the task pane takes up too much space on screen, click its Close button (the X) to remove it.*

2. Estimate the task duration.

Project initially estimates the task duration as 1 day. You can change the duration to some other value by typing the new duration value. You can also use the buttons at the right end of the Duration box to incrementally adjust the duration. Notice that a question mark (?) appears beside the estimate. That is to show that the estimate is an estimated, or tentative, figure. Unless you know precisely when a task will begin and end, make it an estimated task. That way, Project can adjust the amount of time needed to complete the task as necessary.

Table 3-1 lists the abbreviations available for different time measurements. You can use these as you enter the task durations.

MEASUREMENT	MEANING
m	minutes
h	hours
d	days
ed	elapsed days
w	weeks
mo	months

Table 3-1 Time abbreviations available for duration specifications.

3. Repeat actions 1 and 2 for the other tasks.

You need to repeat actions 1 through 2 for each of the other tasks on your to-do list. Figure 3-2 shows an example project schedule that summarizes the work required to write a book after each task is recorded.

Notice that Project assigns a number to each task. Later, when you describe task dependencies, these numbers will become especially important. Notice as well how the bars on the calendar reflect the Duration times. To change your view of the Calendar, click the Zoom In and Zoom Out toolbar buttons. With each click, you either focus on a narrow stretch of time or expand the calendar to see "the big picture."

Figure 3-2 The Microsoft Project window with all the tasks on the to-do list recorded.

NOTE *If you have a recurring task—for example, a weekly meeting—that you want to enter in a project schedule, don't enter that task following the actions described here. Instead, use the Recurring Task command described in the section "Recording Recurring Tasks."*

TIP *To see only tasks and not the calendar as well, choose the View menu's More Views command to open the More Views dialog box, select Task Sheet, and then click the Apply button.*

Handling Tasks and Subtasks

The simple project shown in Figure 3-2 is easy enough to understand because it requires only a handful of tasks. In many real-life situations, however, tasks need to be grouped under summary tasks. This way, you get a better idea of what needs to be done.

Step 3 Schedule Project Tasks   **43**

Take the example book-publishing project. As shown in Figure 3-3, you might want to group the first four tasks under a Write the Book summary task, the fifth and sixth tasks under a Print the Book summary task, and the seventh and eighth tasks under a Sell the Book summary task. In effect, you create three summary tasks and eight subtasks.

Figure 3-3   The Microsoft Project window with all summary tasks and subtasks showing.

Here are instructions for creating and managing summary tasks and subtasks:

- Selecting a row on the Gantt chart: Click a row number on the left side of the chart to select a row. To select several rows, drag the pointer across row numbers. You can tell when rows have been selected because they are highlighted on screen.

- Creating a new row: Select the row that the new row will go above. Then press the Ins key, right-click, and choose New Task on the drop-down menu, or choose the Insert menu's New Task command.

- Creating a summary task: After you have created a new row, enter the summary task name in the Task Name box.

- Grouping subtasks below a summary task: Drag the pointer over row numbers to select each subtask that falls under the summary task. Then right-click and choose Indent on the drop-down menu or click the Indent toolbar button (you will find this button on the Formatting toolbar). Project boldfaces summary tasks to distinguish them from tasks (and subtasks). Notice on the calendar how the time duration of summary tasks is marked with a black line, not a blue bar.

- Moving tasks around in the Gantt chart: Click a row number to select a task. Then drag the number upward or downward to change its location in the Gantt chart.

- Showing and hiding subtasks: Click the Show Subtasks or Hide Subtasks toolbar button to show or hide subtasks in the Gantt chart. You can also click the plus sign (+) or minus sign (-) next to a summary task name or show or hide its subtasks.

Figure 3-3 shows how the book-publishing project schedule looks after adding some summary tasks. Note that Project places any new tasks you add at the same level as the preceding task. This means that if the preceding task is a subtask, you'll want to first identify the new task as a summary task by selecting the task and then clicking the Outdent toolbar button.

NOTE *You don't need to enter durations for summary tasks because Project determines the duration based on the critical path of the subtasks.*

Recording Recurring Tasks

You can enter most of the tasks in a project by entering them one at a time. Some tasks, however, fall in the "recurring" category. They occur weekly, monthly, or at an irregular interval. To enter those tasks, take the following actions:

1. Choose the Insert menu's Recurring Task command.

Project displays the Recurring Task Information dialog box, as shown in Figure 3-4.

Figure 3-4   The Recurring Task Information dialog box.

2. Enter the task description.

Type the task description in the Task Name box.

3. Estimate the task duration.

Type a value in the Duration box to make an initial estimate of the task duration.

NOTE   *Table 3-1 lists the abbreviations available for different time measurements.*

4. Use the Recurrence Pattern option buttons to indicate how often the task recurs.

Depending on which Recurrence Pattern option button you select, Project displays additional boxes and buttons next so you can define the recurring task. In Figure 3-4, for example, the Weekly option button is selected. Project displays boxes for indicating whether the task occurs every week (as opposed to, say, every third week) and on which day of the week.

5. Use the Range Of Recurrence option buttons and boxes to indicate the length of time the task recurs.

You can use the Start and End By buttons and boxes to specify a task that recurs within a certain period of time. Or, you can use the Start and End After buttons and boxes to specify a task that recurs a specific number of times.

6. Click OK.

After you've described the recurring task, click OK. Project adds it to your project schedule. Recurring tasks are marked in Gantt Chart view by a clipboard icon and double-arrow icons. What's more, by clicking the plus sign next to the task's name, you can see when each recurring task is to occur.

NOTE *Use task notes to document additional information about a task. To add a task note to a task, double-click the task so that Project displays the Task Information dialog box and click the Notes tab, if necessary.*

Why Task Duration Errors May Not Matter

One important factor to understand as you estimate task durations are the interrelationships between durations of tasks. Errors in your duration estimates may change the critical path and the project duration—but often not to the extent you might guess. Errors tend to cancel each other out.

For example, assume you will manage a simple project with only three tasks. Further assume that there's a 33% chance each task will take a month, a 33% chance each task will take two months, and a 33% chance each task will take three months.

In this situation, inexperienced project managers tend to make one of two mistakes when setting their task durations. The optimists assume they will complete each task in a month and, therefore, the project in three months. The pessimists assume they will complete each task in three months and, therefore, the project in nine months.

Unfortunately, both the approaches have only a small probability of matching reality. With three tasks, each with three possible durations, 27 different combinations of task durations exist. The probability that all three tasks will be completed in a month is only one chance in 27. Similarly, the probability that all three tasks will take three months is one chance in 27. Both of those outcomes represent less than a 4% probability.

What should you do? Use the median estimate of the task duration—and then add just a bit of cushion. In the simple example described here, there's also only a small 4% chance that each task will take exactly two months. But using two-month task durations still makes most sense because some of the time that one of the tasks takes three months, one of the other tasks will take one month. Errors in duration estimates tend to cancel each other out. In fact, out of the 27 different combinations of task durations for the simple project described here, there are seven chances that the project will take six months, six chances the project will take five months, and six chances that the project will take seven months. By using the average duration estimates and then adding a little extra, say a month, most project duration possibilities are covered. The probability that the project described here can be completed in seven months or less is 23 chances out of 27, or 85%.

Fine-Tuning Duration Values

You can fine-tune the duration estimates that you provide in several ways. You can indicate that a duration is only an estimate, for example. You can also change the start and finish dates. To fine-tune the duration values you entered for a task, double-click the task. In the Task Information dialog box, click the General tab, if necessary. The Task Information dialog box is shown in Figure 3-5. From here, you can change duration values.

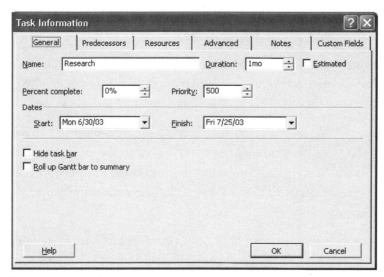

Figure 3-5 The General tab of the Task Information dialog box.

In most cases, task durations *are* estimates. You might want to use the Estimated flag, then, to identify only a certain category of estimated durations. For example, you might use the Estimated flag to identify task durations that haven't been reviewed in relation to the resources required to complete the task.

TIP *You can change a task's duration without opening the Task Information dialog box. To do so, move the pointer to the calendar and place it over the right side of the bar that shows how long tasks take. When you see the arrow, click and start dragging.*

Identifying Task Dependencies

After you list the tasks in a project, the next step is to describe the dependencies between tasks. Establishing dependencies is simply a matter of identifying which tasks precede or succeed other tasks.

Returning to the example of a book-publishing project, obviously you must research the topic before you can create an outline for a book, and you create an outline before you write the book (at least if the book is to be reasonably well organized). You must write the manuscript before you can edit and revise it. The sequence of tasks is as follows: Research, Create Outline, Rough Draft, Edit, Desktop Publish, Print, Distribute, Promote.

Linking Tasks

To identify a task dependency, you enter a number in the Predecessors box in the Gantt chart, as shown in Figure 3-6. In the example of the book-publishing project, you enter *2* in the Predecessors box of the Create Outline task because Research is task number 2 and you need to do the research before creating the outline.

Figure 3-6 A simple book-publishing project with a predecessor task specified for the Create Outline task.

Project offers a couple of different ways to link tasks and establish their dependencies:

- Enter a number in the Predecessors box: Identify a task with a predecessor task and scroll to display the Predecessors column. Besides scrolling, you can display the Predecessors column by dragging the border of the Task table to the right. Next, enter the number of the predecessor task in the Predecessors box. Task numbers appear in the leftmost column of the Gantt chart.

- Click the Link Tasks toolbar button: Select the predecessor task by clicking its number in the Gantt chart. Next, hold down the Ctrl key and select the task that will begin as soon as the predecessor task is complete. With both tasks selected, click the Link Tasks toolbar button.

As you identify predecessors, Project recalculates task start and finish dates. The program also draws arrows in the calendar to show you how one task precedes or succeeds another.

> **TIP** *Some tasks require more than one predecessor. To indicate that a task requires multiple predecessors, separate the task numbers with commas. For example, to tell Project that both the Research and Create Outline tasks need to be completed before the Rough Draft task can start, enter 2,3 in the Rough Draft Predecessors box.*

> **NOTE** *Project assumes that a predecessor task must finish before a successor task can start. Project also assumes that as soon as the predecessor finishes, the successor can start immediately. However, you can tell Project to make other assumptions. Appendix B, "Deal with Project Complexity," explains how to do this in its discussion of other types of predecessor-successor relationships.*

Removing Task Dependencies

To remove a task dependency, take the following actions:

1. **Select the first task with the incorrect predecessor, or prerequisite, task.**

   You can select a task for which you want to remove a predecessor by clicking it.

2. **Edit the contents of the Predecessors box.**

   Edit the incorrect predecessor task number or replace the number. You enter and edit information in a Predecessors box in the same way that you enter and edit information in any text box.

Handling Tasks that Overlap

Suppose you have two options for specifying dependencies for tasks that partially overlap. Generally, it is best to divide the task into two or more tasks and link the individual parts. In the case of the book-publishing project, for example, you would divide the writing task into individual chapters so that some of the writing could overlap the editing. This way, you could write a few chapters and pass them off for editing as you continued to write. However, for tasks that aren't easily divisible, you can also include lag-time between the tasks. To do so, take the following actions:

1. **Double-click the dependent task.**

   Project displays the Task Information dialog box for the task.

2. **Click the Predecessors tab.**

   Figure 3-7 shows the Predecessors tab of the Task Information dialog box.

Figure 3-7   Making tasks overlap.

3. **Specify the overlap between tasks using the Lag box.**

   Either enter a negative value in the Lag box or click the down-arrow on the right side of the Lag box to reduce the lag from the default of 0.

Adding Lag Time between Tasks

Some projects require lag time between tasks. For example, if your task is baking a loaf of bread, you need to plan for the time it takes for the bread to rise after you knead it. Project offers two options for handling lag time. Generally, the best technique is to create a separate task to account for the lag. For a bread-baking project, you would include an hour-long Let Rise task. However, you could also add a lag between the Kneading task and the task that comes after letting the bread rise, namely punching down the dough. To do so, you would double-click the Punch Down Dough task, click the Predecessors tab in the Task Information dialog box, and enter *60m* in the Lag box.

Splitting Tasks

It so happens that sometimes you or your colleagues have to start work on a task, abandon it temporarily, and resume it later on. For those occasions, Project gives you the opportunity to split a task.

Take these actions to split a task:

1. **Switch to Gantt Chart view, if necessary.**
2. **Click the Split Task toolbar button on the Standard toolbar.**

    The Split Task box appears onscreen.
3. **Gently move the mouse pointer—it looks like a right-pointing arrow—on the calendar over the task you want to split, and click and drag to split the task.**

    Drag the mouse pointer to the right. Project enters dots to show where the task has been split.

If you need to unsplit a task, move the pointer over the calendar to where the split occurs. Then click and drag to close the gap.

Understanding the Types of Dependencies

Most dependencies are Finish-to-Start (FS). In other words, the start of one task begins as soon as its predecessor finishes. However, Project offers a few other dependency types. Table 3-2 describes them and offers examples of when they are used.

DEPENDENCY	USED FOR
Start-to-Finish (SF)	When the start of the successor task drives the timing of the end of the predecessor task. For example, if you make improvements to a production facility, closing it temporarily, you want to shut down the backup facility only when the main production facility can resume operations.
Start-to-Start (SS)	When two tasks must start at the same time. For example, you need two resources to meet and grant approval for two processes to begin as soon as possible. If one person is delayed, you need to delay the start of both tasks.
Finish-to-Finish (FF)	When the end of tasks should be linked so they finish at exactly the same time. For example, if you make two improvements to a building that require inspection by a service that charges an expensive per-visit fee, you want to make sure that both improvements finish at the same time so they can be inspected in one visit. If one finishes later, then the other must as well so that the inspection visit can be rescheduled.

Table 3-2 Dependency types available in Project.

To set the type of dependency, double-click the task and click the Predecessors tab in the Task Information dialog box. Then select a dependency type from the Type drop-down list box.

NOTE *You can set dependency types only in the Task Information dialog box. If you link tasks using the other methods, Project assumes that the tasks should be start-to-finish dependencies.*

Adding Other Scheduling Goals and Constraints

For many tasks, you don't need to do anything more than provide a name and the duration and then list the predecessor tasks. However, you may want to identify important project milestones—perhaps so you can more easily report project progress to stakeholders. In some cases, you may also want to more accurately describe scheduling constraints.

Adding Milestones

A common project-management convention is to add milestones to the project. A milestone represents a marker that stakeholders can use to tell whether the project is progressing at the right pace. In Project, a milestone is simply a task with no duration. As shown in Figure 3-8, milestones are marked in the calendar by diamonds and dates. An arrow shows the predecessor task whose completion signals that the milestone has been reached.

Figure 3-8 The Microsoft Project window with two milestones.

To add a milestone to a project, identify the task in the Gantt chart whose completion will coincide with the milestone. You will make this task the milestone's predecessor. Next, create a new task in the normal way, but enter 0 in the Duration box. In the Predecessor box, enter the number of the task whose completion signals arrival of the milestone.

> **TIP** *Remember that you can move tasks higher or lower in the Gantt chart by dragging their numbers up or down. For convenience, place milestone tasks directly below their predecessors so that milestones are easier to identify.*

NOTE *You don't have to use milestones. You can use important tasks—or their completion dates—as markers for monitoring progress.*

Adding Constraint Dates for Deadlines and Priority Tasks

Project lets you add two scheduling constraints to your project: deadlines, before which a task must be completed, and constraint types, which let you indicate scheduling characteristics such as the fact that a task should start as soon as possible or as late as possible.

To place a scheduling constraint on a task, take the following actions:

1. **Double-click the task in the Gantt chart.**

   Project opens the Task Information dialog box, as shown in Figure 3-9.

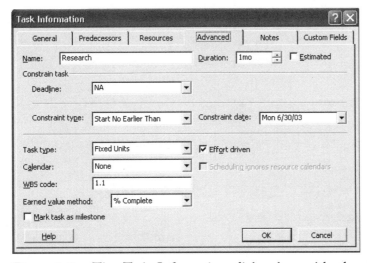

Figure 3-9 The Task Information dialog box with the Advanced tab showing a deadline.

2. **Click the Advanced tab.**

3. **Specify a deadline, if necessary.**

   If a task must be completed by a specific date, enter this date in the Deadline box.

   When you specify a deadline, Project compares the estimated finish date for a task to the deadline. If the deadline you enter falls before the estimated finish date, Project alerts you to this problem by flagging the task in the Gantt view with an exclamation mark.

Deadlines are marked on the calendar by a down-pointing arrow. Move the pointer over the arrow, and a box appears to tell you when the deadline falls.

4. Specify a starting or ending date constraint, if necessary.

By default, Project schedules tasks to start as soon as possible but only after any predecessor tasks are complete.

You can change this scheduling rule by choosing a constraint from the Constraint Type drop-down list box. For example, you can indicate that Project should schedule some task to start as late as possible but without delaying the projected completion date. (To do this, you choose the As Late As Possible entry from the Constraint Type list box.)

The Constraint Type list box also provides a series of self-explanatory constraints that let you indicate that a task should start or finish by a specified date. For example, you can specify that a task must start by a particular date. To specify this date, you use the Constraint Date box.

NOTE *Although adding constraint dates to tasks often complicates a schedule, such constraints are sometimes necessary. For example, a contract may state that some task must be started or finished by a specific date.*

NOTE *You can tell when a constraint has been placed on a task by looking at the first column of the Gantt chart. In that column, you see a tiny calendar. Move the pointer over the calendar and a pop-up message describes the constraint.*

Resolving Dependency-Constraint Conflicts

When you attach a constraint date to a task, you often create conflicts between dependencies and the constraint date. Suppose, for example, that task B can start only after task A finishes and that task A finishes on June 1. If you set a constraint date that says task B must start on May 1, your dependency and constraint date conflict.

Project looks for and alerts you to conflicts between dependencies and constraints. To notify you of a conflict, the program displays Planning Wizard dialog boxes like the one in Figure 13-10. These dialog boxes help you work out conflicts.

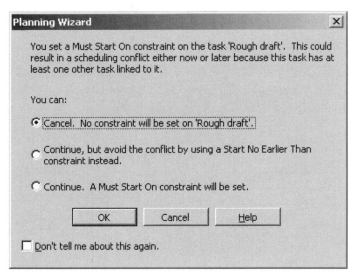

Figure 3-10 The Planning Wizard alerts you to a dependency-constraint conflict.

One way to handle conflicts is to simply cancel the creation of a dependency or constraint that creates the conflict. You do this by selecting the Cancel option button.

Another way to deal with the conflict is to acknowledge it and tell Project to fix it. You do this by selecting a Continue option button.

Project "fixes" a scheduling conflict by ignoring the dependency and using only the constraint date in its scheduling. Which means, of course, that you need to be very careful about how you use these scheduling exceptions because scheduling exceptions usually override the basic logic of a schedule.

Project may also suggest a "flexible constraint;" in this example a Start No Earlier Than constraint. The task is constrained to the specified date, unless the linked task forces this task's dates to change. The linked task still takes precedence over the task's dates. The flexible constraints Project suggests will differ, depending on the type of constraint you attempt to use, and whether your project is scheduled from the start date or the finish date.

If you don't want Project to fix scheduling constraints by overriding dependencies and focusing exclusively on the constraint date, take the following actions:

1. **Choose the Tools menu's Options command, and click the Schedule tab.**

   Project displays the Schedule tab of the Options dialog box, as shown in Figure 3-11.

2. Clear the Tasks Will Always Honor Their Constraint Dates check box.

After you've made this specification, click OK. Project closes the dialog box.

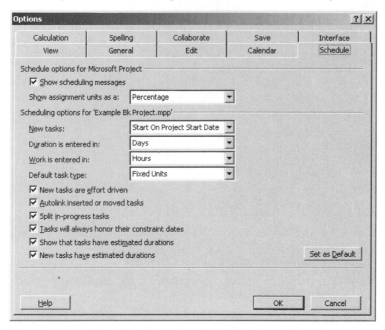

Figure 3-11 The Schedule tab of the Options dialog box.

Summary

After you've identified and scheduled your project tasks, taking into account task dependencies and constraints, you've actually accomplished the first of the two major planning steps related to organizing a project. The second major planning step is described in "Step 4: Identify and Allocate Resources."

Step 4

IDENTIFY AND ALLOCATE RESOURCES

Tasks Required to Complete the Step
- Allocating resources
- Fine-tuning duration calculations for resources
- Creating different calendars for groups of resources
- Editing calendars for individual resources
- Reviewing resource allocations
- Leveling resources
- Assigning costs to resources
- Sharing resources

For most projects, you need to assign and then monitor resources such as people and equipment. This is the fourth step in managing a project using Microsoft Project 2002.

Allocating Resources

Resources are the workers and tools needed to accomplish a task. In simple situations, identifying and assigning resources to a project is easy. You can simultaneously identify and allocate resources simply by entering resource names in the Resource Names column of the Gantt chart.

NOTE *Resources also include any equipment or machinery your project requires, such as a bulldozer, a helicopter, or a crane, as described in the next section.*

Assigning Resources

To assign resources to tasks, take the following actions:

1. **Select the task to which you want to assign a resource.**

   To do this most easily, simply click the Resource Names box of the task while you are in Gantt Chart view. Resource Names is the sixth column.

2. **Name the resource.**

   To do this, type the resource name or a short description using the Resource Names box, as shown in Figure 4-1. You might, for example, use a person's first name if you have only a short list of people resources: Alice, Bob, Carmen, and so on.

   You can also open the drop-down list and choose a resource that way.

   If your project requires the efforts of many people, use first initials in combination with last names: Dellington, Nbonaparte, and so on. If a task requires more than one resource, separate resource names with commas.

Figure 4-1   The project after resources are assigned.

3. **Repeat actions 1 and 2 for each task to which you want to assign resources.**

   Assign resources to all tasks and subtasks, but not milestones and not summary tasks. As a practical matter, resource allocations often represent guesses on your part until you can confirm that a resource is available.

   TIP *To assign the same resource a second time, don't bother typing it in. Instead, click the down arrow in the Resource Names box and choose a resource from the drop-down list.*

Specifying Parts and Equipment as Resources

As mentioned earlier, not only can you add human resources to tasks but you can also assign materials and equipment to tasks. To do so, enter the material or equipment for the task in the Resource Names column of the Gantt chart in the same way that you enter a human resource. Then take the following actions:

1. **Choose the View menu's Resource Sheet command.**

   Project displays the Resource Sheet listing the project's resources.

2. **Click the Type column for the material resource, and select Material from the drop-down list box.**

3. **Press the Enter key.**

   Project displays a message box alerting you that you're changing the resource type.

4. **Click OK.**

   Project adjusts the columns of the Resource Sheet to make them appropriate for costs of goods rather than services, as shown in Figure 4-2.

Figure 4-2 Adding a material good as a resource.

5. **In the Material Label column, enter the units by which you'll specify the value required.**

   For example, if you enter *printing press time* as a material resource, you would enter *hours*.

6. **Specify the cost of the good.**

   If you're paying rent to use the good, enter a value in the Std. Rate column. If the good costs a flat fee, enter the cost in the Cost/Use column.

NOTE *If your project uses a currency for cost amounts different from the currency settings described in the Regional Settings tool on your computer, choose the Tools menu's Options command and click the View tab. Then enter the currency symbol your project uses and the number of decimal digits, and specify the placement of the symbol in regard to the value. For example, if your project costs are in British Pounds, you would enter £ in the Symbol box and select 1 £ from the Placement drop-down list box. To enter common currency symbols into the Symbol box, use the Windows Character Map utility.*

7. **When you're finished, choose the View menu's Gantt Chart command to return to the Gantt chart.**

    Notice that Project has placed the value 1 in square brackets after the good's name in the Resource Names column, assuming that the quantity of the good required for the task is one. To specify a different quantity, change the value in the square brackets.

TIP *To see only work resources or material resources, choose Resources - Material or Resources - Work on the Filter drop-down menu. You will find this menu on the Formatting toolbar.*

Removing Resources

You can easily remove resources you've assigned. Project offers a couple of different ways to do this:

- Starting in the Gantt chart: Clear the Resource Names box in the Gantt Chart view. To do so, select the Resource Names box, select the resource's name, and press the Delete key.

- From the Assign Resources dialog box: In the Gantt chart, click the name of the resource you want to remove. Then click the Assign Resources toolbar button or choose the Tools menu's Assign Resources command. Project displays the Assign Resources dialog box, as shown in Figure 4-3. Under Resource Name, click the name of the resource you want to remove and then click the Remove button.

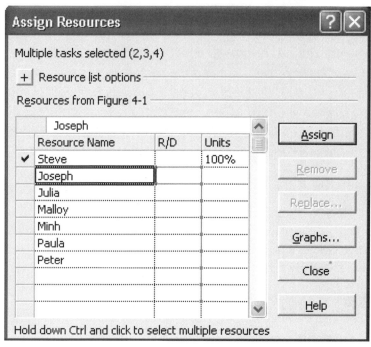

Figure 4-3 The Assign Resources dialog box.

TIP *In a project with many resources, locating a resource in the Assign Resources dialog box can be difficult. Click the plus-sign button next to Resource List Options. Then, in the Filter By drop-down list, look over the options for filtering, or limiting the number of, resource names in the dialog box. Choose an option and you will have fewer resource names to sort through.*

Substituting One Resource for Another

You can replace resources by way of the Assign Resources command and its dialog box. And you can also do it by way of the Resource Names drop-down list in Gantt chart view. Here are the two techniques for substituting one resource for another:

- In Gantt chart view: Display the resource that needs substituting, open the drop-down menu in the Resource Names box, and choose a different resource.

- Assign Resources command: Click the Assign Resources toolbar button or choose the Tools menu's Assign Resources command to open the Assign Resources dialog box (see Figure 4-3). Next, click outside the dialog box and, on the Gantt chart, select the task for which you want to substitute a resource. Then, back in the dialog box, select the name of the assigned resource you want to replace and click the Replace button. You see the Replace Resource dialog box, as shown in Figure 4-4. Select the new replacement resource and click OK.

Figure 4-4 The Replace Resource dialog box.

Fine-Tuning Duration Calculations for Resources

By default, when you specify a task duration in Project, Project assumes the task requires a specified amount of effort. If you indicate that some task will take four days, Project assumes you mean the task requires four days of work, or effort. Project calls effort-based durations *fixed-unit durations*. Tasks with fixed-unit durations are called *fixed-unit tasks*.

With fixed-unit tasks, adding more resources results in the task finishing more quickly. Suppose, for example, that a fixed unit task has a four-day duration. With one person assigned to the task, the task takes four days to complete. With two people assigned, the task takes two days to complete. With four people, one day.

In addition to fixed-unit durations, Project lets you specify two other types of duration: *fixed duration* and *fixed work*.

A fixed-duration task indicates that the passage of time itself is required. In a construction project, for example, concrete may actually require the passage of time in order to cure. If you indicate that a concrete foundation requires four days to cure, the task Cure concrete takes four days no matter what resources you assign.

A fixed-work task amounts to a hybrid of fixed-unit tasks and fixed-duration tasks. With a fixed-work task, you can't accelerate the task's completion by adding resources. But as you add resources, you reduce the percentage of the resource devoted to the task. For example, if a fixed-work task has a duration of four days and you assign one person, the task requires all, or 100%, of the person's time for four days. If you assign two people, however, while the project still takes four days to complete, it requires only half, or 50%, of the people's time over those four days. If you assign four people, the project still takes four days, but it now requires only one quarter, or 25%, of the people's time.

To specify how Project should calculate the duration for a task, take the following actions:

1. Double-click the task.

Project opens the Task Information dialog box. Click the Advanced tab to show the Advanced tab of options, as shown in Figure 4-5.

Figure 4-5 The Advanced tab of the Task Information dialog box.

2. **Select the appropriate duration calculation method from the Task Type drop-down list.**

   Choose Fixed Units (the default), Fixed Duration, or Fixed Work.

3. **Indicate whether Project should recalculate the time it takes to complete the task or the effort assigned to the task.**

   Select or clear the Effort Driven check box to indicate whether Project should calculate the duration based on the effort or the effort based on the duration.

   NOTE *A fixed-work task is by definition effort driven, so the Effort Driven check box is always selected for this duration calculation method. You have the option of clearing the Effort Driven check box only for fixed-duration or fixed-unit tasks.*

   The Effort Driven check box's effect can seem confusing at first, but it follows these rules to adjust the duration and effort:

   - If the Effort Driven check box is selected for a fixed-unit task, Project recalculates the task duration when you change the resources assigned to the task, but Project doesn't recalculate the resources assigned to the task when you change the duration.

   - If the Effort Driven check box is *not* selected for a fixed-unit task, Project recalculates the task duration when you change the resources assigned to the task and recalculates the resources assigned to the task when you change the duration.

   - If the Effort Driven check box is selected for a fixed-duration task, Project recalculates the resources assigned to the task when you change the resources assigned to the task, but Project doesn't recalculate the duration when you change the resources and it doesn't recalculate the resources assigned to the task when you change the duration.

   - If the Effort Driven check box is *not* selected for a fixed-duration task, Project doesn't recalculate the resources assigned to the task when you change the resources assigned to the task, and it doesn't recalculate the duration when you change the resources assigned to the task.

To specify that a resource work only part-time on a task, take the following actions:

1. **Display the project in Gantt Chart view.**

   If necessary, choose the View menu's Gantt Chart option to display the project in Gantt Chart view.

2. **Select the Resource Names column for the task to which you want to assign part-time resources.**

   Project displays any resources you've assigned to the task in the Entry bar at the top of the Gantt chart.

3. **After a resource's name, enter the percentage of time the resource will work on the task in square brackets.**

   Do not leave a space between the resource's name and the brackets. Figure 4-6 shows two resources assigned to work on a task for 20% of a full day's work as specified by the project's calendar. If you specified the task as Fixed Units or Fixed Work, Project recalculates the task duration.

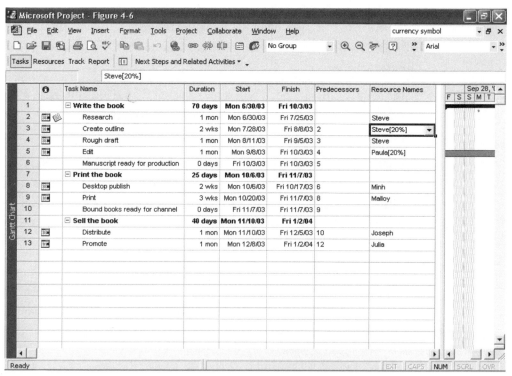

Figure 4-6   Specifying that a resource works part-time on a task.

Creating Different Calendars for Groups of Resources

"Step 2: Describe the Project" describes how to create a base calendar for a project or a company. However, when groups of resources work different schedules, you may want to create a specific calendar for each group and assign the resources in each group to a different calendar. For example, a group of resources may be on assignment and therefore unavailable for a certain month of the year. Likewise, people who work in international divisions may celebrate different holidays and work different schedules.

NOTE *Create new calendars only for groups of resources who share similar schedules, not for individuals. The section "Editing Calendars for Individual Resources" later in this Step describes how you can personalize calendars for individuals.*

To create a new calendar for a group of resources, take the following actions:

1. **Choose the Tools menu's Change Working Time command.**

   Project displays the Change Working Time dialog box, as shown in Figure 4-7.

Figure 4-7 The Change Working Time dialog box.

2. **Indicate you want to create a new calendar.**

   Click the New button. Project displays the Create New Base Calendar dialog box, as shown in Figure 4-8.

Figure 4-8 The Create New Base Calendar dialog box.

3. **Name the new base calendar.**

   Enter the name you want to use for the project calendar. For example, you might enter *Seasonal Crew* or *Seattle Division*.

4. **Copy an existing schedule's information as a starting point.**

   Click the Make A Copy Of option button, select one of the existing calendars of working and nonworking time from the drop-down list box, and then click OK.

5. **Identify nonworking days.**

   To identify nonworking days not already included on the base calendar, use the calendar shown in the Change Working Time dialog box to display the month with the holidays. After the month shows, press and hold down the Ctrl key and click each day that you want to mark as a nonworking day.

6. **Describe exceptions to the typical workday or workweek.**

   To identify any exceptions to the typical workday or workweek, use the calendar shown in the Change Working Time dialog box to show the month with the exceptions.

   After the month shows, press and hold down the Ctrl key and click each of the days with the exception.

   After you do this, click the Nondefault Working Time option button and use the From and To boxes to describe the exception.

   NOTE *In the Change Working Time dialog box is a legend that explains how working, nonworking, and nondefault working times appear on the calendar.*

7. **Save your calendar.**

   Click OK to save your calendar changes.

8. **Attach resources to the correct calendar.**

   Display the Resource Sheet (choose the View menu's Resource Sheet command) and scroll over to the Base Calendar column. Select the correct base calendar for each resource, as shown in Figure 4-9.

Figure 4-9 Selecting the correct base calendar for each resource.

Editing Calendars for Individual Resources

By default, Project uses your base calendars for showing which resources are available. If the base calendar shows that June 1 is a working day, Project assumes that the resources to which the calendar applies are available on June 1. If the project calendar shows that June is a nonworking day, Project assumes that resources aren't available that day.

Sometimes, however, you need to edit a calendar specifically for an individual resource, usually a person. For instance, you can edit a calendar to show when a person goes on vacation or takes a leave of absence. In essence, you create a resource calendar by making a copy of the base calendar and then making any needed changes.

NOTE *If you don't want to edit calendars for individual resources, you can also manually organize your projects in such a way that you don't rely on a worker the same week she is on vacation or on a piece of machinery the same week it's being serviced.*

To customize a calendar for a particular resource, take the following actions:

1. Display the Resource Sheet.

Choose the View menu's Resource Sheet command. Project displays the Resource Sheet.

2. Double-click the resource.

Project displays the Resource Information dialog box for the resource. Click the Working Time tab to display the set of options shown in Figure 4-10.

Figure 4-10 The Working Time tab of the Resource Information dialog box.

3. Verify the resource's base calendar.

Use the Base Calendar drop-down list to select the calendar that most closely matches the resource's schedule.

4. Identify the resource's nonworking days.

To identify nonworking days, such as vacation and personal leave days, use the calendar shown on the Working Time tab. You can move backward or forward in the calendar by dragging the slider on the vertical scroll bar on the right side of the calendar.

After the month shows, press and hold down the Ctrl key and click each day that you want to mark as a nonworking day.

After you've done this, click the Nonworking Time option button. Figure 4-10 shows the third week of July 2003 marked as nonworking days.

5. **Describe exceptions to the typical workday or workweek.**

   To identify any exceptions to the typical workday or workweek, use the calendar to display the month with the exception. Then press and hold down the Ctrl key and click each of the days with the exception.

   After you do this, click the Nondefault Working Time option button and use the From and To boxes to describe the exception. Figure 4-11 shows July 11, 2003, as a four-hour workday, which is an exception to the typical eight-hour workday.

Figure 4-11 The Change Working Time dialog box—this time showing an exception to the usual eight-hour workday.

NOTE *The Change Working Time dialog box provides a legend that explains how working, nonworking, and nondefault working times appear on the calendar.*

6. **If necessary, specify the worker as seasonal or part-time.**

   Click the General tab of the Resource Information dialog box. Use the Available From and Available To boxes to specify the range of dates the resource is available. Use the Units box to specify the amount of the resource available as a percentage. For example, 50% would be a half-time resource, 67% would be a two-thirds time resource. Figure 4-12 shows the General tab of the Resource Information dialog box filled out for a high school student.

Step 4 *Identify and Allocate Resources* **73**

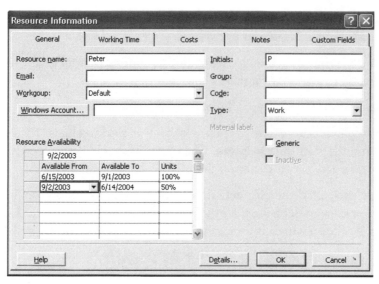

Figure 4-12 Specifying worker availability.

7. **Save your calendar changes.**

   Click OK to save your resource calendar changes.

8. **Repeat actions 2 through 6, as necessary.**

   To create resource calendars for other resources, repeat actions 2 through 6 as necessary.

Reviewing Resource Allocations

After you allocate resources and, if necessary, verify that Project's duration calculations are working correctly, you should review the allocations.

Obviously, you want to make sure that people aren't overscheduled. Overtime, apart from the personal burden it places on team members, also creates project risks because it means there's never any cushion in people's schedules.

You also often want to make sure that people stay busy. A schedule in which someone works sporadically doesn't work well for the individual or the project.

Using the Resource Sheet View

Often, you can most easily review the resource allocations you've made by using the Resource Sheet view, as shown in Figure 4-13. It shows the hours each resource is scheduled to work. To view a Resource Sheet for the open project file, choose the View menu's Resource Sheet command. Notice in the figure that some of the resources are overallocated.

Figure 4-13 The Resource Sheet.

NOTE *Project identifies any overallocated resources by placing an exclamation point in the Indicator column of the Resource Sheet. On your monitor, Project also flags these overallocated resources by displaying them in red.*

Step 4 Identify and Allocate Resources

Using the Resource Graph View

Another handy view is the Resource Graph, shown in Figure 4-14. It shows resource usage in a bar chart. Regular hours are shown in blue (on a color monitor or printer) and overtime hours in red. To view a Resource Graph for the open project file, choose the View menu's Resource Graph command.

Figure 4-14 The Resource Graph view.

To scroll through the resources, slide the scroll bar in the left area of the Resource Graph view. This area names the resource depicted in the Resource Graph.

To scroll through the calendar, slide the scroll bar in the right area of the Resource Graph view. This area shows the bar chart of resource allocation.

Using the Resource Usage View

Still one other view that depicts resources is the Resource Usage view, shown in Figure 4-15. It shows resource usage in a table by task. To view a Resource Usage view for the open project file, choose the View menu's Resource Usage command.

Figure 4-15 The Resource Usage view.

NOTE *To collapse the tasks detail for a resource so that only the resource's total assigned hours show, click the button marked with the minus (-) symbol. To later expand the tasks, click the button marked with the plus (+) symbol. Project replaces the minus button with the plus button and vice versa when you click it.*

Leveling Resources

Many projects show overallocated resources—yet they do so without creating problems. Slightly overscheduled resources can sometimes work overtime. Occasionally, despite what the schedule shows, the project stays on track even if work slides around a little: work that the schedule shows should be done on Tuesday through Thursday can instead be spread from Monday through Friday, for example.

When the resource overallocation isn't acceptable, you have two options. You can adjust the schedule manually by adding resources, reducing durations, or eliminating constraints. Or you can tell Project to level resources. Resource leveling means to stretch out a project schedule so that resources are not overallocated.

Leveling Resources Manually

Manual resource leveling works the way you would expect. Your first action may be to review first-guess durations as well as any constraints to see whether durations can be tightened and constraints loosened. Either sort of change can easily fix overallocations.

Your second action is to look at assigning more resources. Instead of using one person, you might try two. Or three. Typically, you lose efficiency at some point by assigning more resources. Still, assigning a team of people is often the best way to complete a project. To reduce resource overallocation by assigning multiple resources, the task duration type must be set to either Fixed Units or Fixed Work and Effort Driven.

NOTE *For more information about these two types of duration, see the earlier section "Fine-Tuning Duration Calculations for Resources."*

Still a third technique for leveling resources is to reorganize the project so the work of a resource is spread over a greater length of time. In computer book publishing, for example, we actually do this by breaking tasks into subtasks (and sometimes breaking subtasks into sub-subtasks). This gambit often lets a resource begin work earlier and finish work later than would otherwise be possible because work can be done concurrently.

For example, in standard book publishing, a book is written and then it is edited. If writing takes three months and editing takes two months and the editing task must follow the writing task, the project duration equals five months. In computer book publishing, however, as a writer finishes an individual chapter (or perhaps a set of chapters), the chapters go to the editor for editing. In this manner, work is scheduled concurrently. As the writer is writing Chapter 3, say, the editor is editing Chapters 1 and 2.

You can schedule concurrently to reduce the time it takes to finish a project, of course. You can also use this concurrent scheduling to finish the project in the same length of time as originally scheduled—except with resource usage spread over longer periods of time. For more information about dividing and linking tasks, refer to "Step 3: Schedule Project Tasks."

Restructuring Projects for Resources

I have tried restructuring a project for purely resource scheduling reasons. For example, the standard book project structure schedules a technical editor to follow the copy editor so that the technical editor also checks the copy editor's changes. We have tried flip-flopping these tasks to make the schedule work better.

In my experience, however, restructuring for resource reasons hasn't work well. Team members get used to a standard structure. Deviating from the standard structure resulted in confusion and mistakes. I was often running several book projects at once, so it was predictably confusing to structure eleven book projects in the traditional way and then structure the twelfth book project in some new way.

But there was another surprise we had with this sort of change: We tended to underestimate the negative effect of such a schedule change on deliverable quality and then also to overestimate the positive effect on the schedule. We thought we were trading an imperceptible reduction in book quality for a nice change in the project schedule. We usually traded imperceptible reductions in the project schedule for sometimes glaring (to us) reductions in the book quality.

Leveling Resources Automatically

Automatic resource leveling stretches out the project by delaying tasks and splitting tasks. When Project delays a task, it simply moves it into the future when the resource is available. When it splits a task, work on the task progresses at various intervals—but only when resources are available.

Limits exist, however, as to what Project can do to level resources. Project won't violate any constraints you've set as it levels resources, for example. For more information about constraints, refer to the section "Adding Other Scheduling Goals and Constraints" in "Step 3: Schedule Project Tasks."

Project also won't delay or split any tasks to which you've assigned a priority of 1000. In other words, you use the priority setting of 1000 to show that a task shouldn't be adjusted in any resource leveling. To set a task priority to 1000 so that it won't be adjusted, double-click the task in the Gantt Chart view (or some other view) to display the Task Information dialog box. Then click the General tab, and enter 1000 in the Priority box.

To level the resources in a project, take the following actions:

1. Choose the Tools menu's Level Resources command.

Project displays the Resource Leveling dialog box, as shown in Figure 4-16.

Figure 4-16 The Resource Leveling dialog box.

2. Choose either Automatic or Manual resource leveling.

You can direct Project to automatically level resources as you work or to level resources only when you choose the Resource Leveling command.

To make this choice, click the appropriate button: Automatic or Manual.

NOTE *Automatic resource leveling is calculation-intense for Project and your personal computer. For large or complex projects, this option may noticeably slow down Project's speed and responsiveness.*

3. Indicate the time interval at which Project should watch for overallocation.

You use the Look For Overallocations drop-down list box to specify, essentially, just what an overallocation is. Is a resource overallocated if it's scheduled for more than eight hours in a day? Forty hours in a week? Sixty minutes in an hour?

By default, Project considers any day in which a resource is scheduled for more than a full day's work (probably eight hours) as a resource overallocation. In this case, the Look For Overallocations box shows Day By Day.

It may be, however, that you can work with a looser definition of overallocation. For example, if an overallocation doesn't really occur unless a resource is scheduled for more than a full week's work in a week, you might select Week By Week.

The Look For Overallocations drop-down list box also provides even looser definitions of overallocations (like Month By Month) as well as tighter definitions of overallocation (Hour By Hour and Minute By Minute).

NOTE *The looser the definition you use for overallocation, the less resource leveling Project performs.*

4. **Optionally, select a range of dates for which Project should level resources.**

   If the Level Entire Project option button is selected, as it is by default, Project will level resources over the entire project schedule.

   You can also limit Project's leveling to a specified period of time. To do this, select the Level option button and then define the range of dates in the From and To boxes.

5. **Specify the order in which Project should consider leveling criteria.**

   The Leveling Order drop-down list box provides three leveling order options: ID Only, Standard, and Priority/Standard.

   The default leveling order is Standard. In this case, Project levels tasks by considering first their predecessor dependencies, then their slack, and then their dates, priorities, and constraints.

   If you select ID Only, Project levels tasks in ascending ID number order and then, if that's not enough, goes on to include other leveling considerations, including predecessor dependencies, slack, dates, priorities, and constraints.

   If you select Priority/Standard, Project first considers the task priorities, then predecessor dependencies, and then slack, dates, and constraints.

6. **Indicate whether Project can move the finish date.**

   If Project can or can't move the finish, or project completion, date, select the Level Only Within Available Slack check box. With this box marked, Project will perform minor adjustments, but it won't do anything that delays a path on the critical path.

7. **Indicate whether Project can individually adjust when a resource works on a task.**

   If Project can individually adjust when a resource works on a task—independent of the work that other resources working on the same task perform—select the Leveling Can Adjust Individual Assignments On A Task check box.

8. **Indicate whether Project can split a task so it occurs at two or more separate times.**

   If Project can split a task so it occurs at different times, select the Leveling Can Create Splits In Remaining Work check box.

9. **Start leveling.**

   After you've described how Project should level the resources, click the Level Now button. Project levels the project's resources.

Undoing Your Resource Leveling

You can reverse the effects of Project's resource leveling in either of two ways: If you've just leveled resources and haven't made other changes to the project, you can choose the Edit menu's Undo Leveling command.

If you've made changes to the project since leveling resources, you can choose the Tools menu's Level Resources command. Then, when Project displays the Resource Leveling dialog box, click the Clear Leveling button.

Assigning Costs to Resources

To assign costs to resources, take the following actions:

1. **Display the Resource Sheet.**

   Choose the View menu's Resource Sheet command. Project displays the Resource Sheet.

2. **Double-click the resource.**

   When Project displays the Resource Information dialog box, click the Costs tab shown in Figure 4-17.

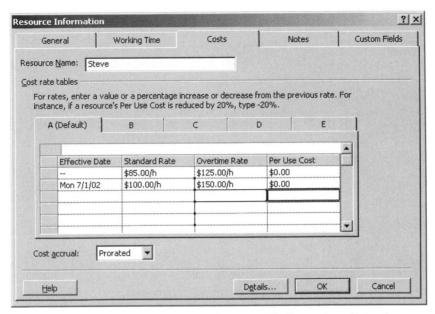

Figure 4-17 The Costs tab in the Resource Information dialog box.

3. **Create a cost rate table for the resource.**

   Describe the cost of the resource by providing the standard hourly rate, an overtime rate, and, if appropriate, any one-time cost or charge associated simply with using the resource.

   If a resource's costs will change at some point in the future, you can also provide this information by adding an effective date and then new standard hourly, overtime hourly, and one-time cost information.

   Figure 4-17 shows the A cost rate schedule for resource "Steve." Through July 1, 2002, the resource's standard cost is $85 per hour, $125 per overtime hour. After July 1, 2002, the resource's standard cost increases to $100 an hour, and the overtime cost increases to $150 an hour.

   TIP *To describe a standard rate for resources, choose the Tools menu's Options command and click the General tab. Enter the standard rates in the Default Standard Rate and Default Overtime Rate boxes.*

4. **Optionally, repeat step 3 to create additional cost rate tables.**

   Project lets you create more than one cost rate table for a resource. Many times, you won't need or want to do this. If your resource produces different costs depending on how it is used, you might choose to set up a separate cost rate table for each type of use.

   An attorney who does both legal research and provides expert testimony, for example, might charge different rates for each type of service. To deal with this, you could use two cost rate tables.

   To create another cost rate table, click the next cost-rate-table tab, and then use it to describe the other cost rate.

5. **Use the Cost Accrual drop-down list box to specify how and when you want resource costs charged to a task.**

   Select Start to calculate the cost for the task as soon as the task begins; select End to calculate the cost when the task is completed; or select Prorated to accrue the cost of the task as the work is completed.

   NOTE *If you set a Per Use Cost for a resource, Project always adds this cost to the task at the start of the task.*

6. **Describe the other resources in the project, as necessary.**

   Repeat actions 2 through 4 to describe each of the other resources in the project.

   TIP *You can also assign a single cost rate table to a resource directly on the Resource Sheet. Just enter values in the Std. Rate, Ovt. Rate, and Cost/Use columns.*

Sharing Resources

If you have several projects (or anticipate additional projects) and want to use a common group of resources for them, you can create a resource pool to share the resources across projects. The convenience of a resource pool is that you enter information about the individual resources only once. Depending on the amount of resource information you enter, creating a shared resource pool can save you a lot of time.

Setting Up a Resource Pool

To set up a resource pool, take the following actions:

1. **Create or save a Project file that contains resource information.**

   If you have already created a project that contains information about resources, open it and save it under a new name. (You don't need to delete the tasks.) If you haven't created a project that contains the resource information you want to share, do so.

   NOTE *Although you technically don't need to create a separate Project file for the resource pool, it usually makes sense to do so, especially in a multi-user environment. Otherwise, when you want to edit the project containing the resource pool, you block others out of working with projects linked to the resource pool.*

2. **Open the Project file that you want to link to the resource pool.**

   Either create a new project or open an existing project.

3. **Choose the Tools menu's Resource Sharing command, and choose the submenu's Share Resources command.**

   Project displays the Share Resources dialog box, as shown in Figure 4-18.

   Figure 4-18 The Share Resources dialog box.

4. **Specify the file with the resource pool.**

   Click the Use Resources option button, and select the file with the resource pool from the From drop-down list box.

5. **Specify what Project should do if it encounters calendar conflicts.**

   Click the Pool Takes Precedence option button to make the calendars in the resource pool file take precedence. Click the Sharer Takes Precedence option button to make the calendars in the active Project file take precedence.

6. **Click OK.**

   Project links the file to the resource pool.

Using a Project File with a Shared Resource Pool

When you later open the project that uses the resource pool, Project displays the Open Resource Pool dialog box, as shown in Figure 4-19.

Figure 4-19 The Open Resource Pool dialog box.

The dialog box contains three options:

- Click the first option button to open the file and the resource pool.

- Click the second option button to open only the file and not the resource pool. If you make changes to resource information while working with the file, Project will not be able to update the resource pool with these changes.

- Click the third option button to create a new master project file with the projects and the resource pool.

Updating a Resource Pool

To update the resource pool if you make changes to resource information in the file, choose the Tools menu's Resource Sharing command and choose the submenu's Update Resource Pool command. If you forget to do this and attempt to close the project file, Project prompts you to update the resource pool.

Unlinking a Resource Pool

To stop sharing resources in a project, open the project, choose the Tools menu's Resources command, and choose the submenu's Share Resources command. Then click the Use Own Resources option button, and click OK.

To unlink a resource pool from multiple projects, take the following actions:

1. **Open the resource pool file.**

   Open this file directly, in read-write mode.

2. **Choose the Tools menu's Resource Sharing command, and choose the submenu's Share Resources command.**

   Project displays the Share Resources dialog box, as shown in Figure 4-20.

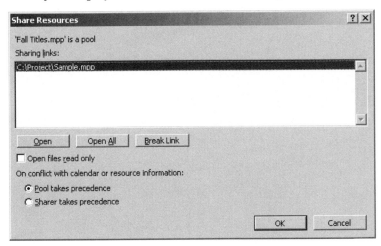

Figure 4-20 The Share Resources dialog box.

3. **Select the projects you want to unlink from the resource pool.**

   The Sharing Links box lists all projects using resources from the resource pool. Select the projects you want to unlink from the resource pool.

4. **Click the Break Link button.**

5. **Click OK.**

Summary

After you've scheduled your project tasks and assigned resources to these tasks, you've accomplished the two major planning steps related to organizing a project. You're now ready to look over what you've done, as described in "Step 5: Review Project Organization."

Step 5

REVIEW PROJECT ORGANIZATION

Tasks Required to Complete the Step
- Outlining your project
- Changing the timescale
- Using filters
- Sorting tasks and resources
- Looking at your project in various views

Now that you've created the basic structure of your project and assigned resources to the various tasks, the time has come to take a good look at it before passing it around to the people and groups who will either be involved in the project or affected by it. With Microsoft Project 2002, you can look at the organization of your project in myriad ways, each designed to focus on a particular aspect. With a simple project, you can often get most of the information you need from the Gantt Chart view. As your projects become more complex, however, you can manipulate them so that you can identify and scrutinize areas that are sure to produce surprises when you least expect them.

Outlining Your Project

You may have noticed in previous steps that one of the first tasks involved in a book-publishing project is creating an outline. Outlining is essential when you're preparing a document of any length, as you probably remember from your high-school language arts classes. An outline provides the structure for organizing your thoughts and presenting them in a coherent manner.

An outline is equally important in project management for the same reason: it provides an ordered structure for the tasks in a project. With an outline, you can group tasks and summarize their associated duration, cost, and resources.

"Step 3: Schedule Project Tasks" looked briefly at how you add summary tasks to a project and in so doing create a simple outline. This step looks at this process in more detail and shows you how to use an outline to manage projects more effectively.

Using Summary Tasks

A *summary task* is a task in a project outline that has subordinate tasks, or *subtasks*. You can create an outline in two ways:

- From the top down, by identifying summary tasks
- From the bottom up, by listing all the subtasks

For example, if you're planning the research work for publishing a book, you might have the following summary tasks:

1. Review existing books.

2. Interview experts.

3. Make field trips.

You can then break out the subtasks that each of these summary tasks involves. The second summary task, Interviewing experts, might involve the following subtasks:

1. Meet with Walter S.

2. Meet with Elfrida R.

3. Meet with Josef A.

Figure 5-1 shows how this summary task and its subtasks look in Project. If you need to refresh your memory about the actions required to enter summary tasks and subtasks, take a look back at Step 3.

Figure 5-1 A summary task and its subtasks.

Sometimes, however, starting with the subtasks and then inserting summary tasks is more useful. In other words, working from the bottom up. Step 3 used this approach to enter the to-do list and then insert summary tasks.

You often need to do this when you're reviewing the organization of your project. For example, you may discover that a subtask involves sub-subtasks and really should be a summary task. As you recall from Step 3, you define summary tasks by entering a task and then indenting the subtasks.

Using the Outlining Tools

Regardless of whether you choose the top-down or bottom-up approach to outlining, you use the tools on the left side of the Formatting toolbar to promote and demote tasks. Figure 5-2 shows the Formatting toolbar.

Figure 5-2 The Formatting toolbar.

Click the Show button on the Formatting toolbar to display more or fewer levels in your outline. For example, if your outline has three levels, clicking Show and then clicking Outline Level 3 or All Subtasks displays all three levels. Clicking Show and then clicking Outline Level 2 displays only the first two levels and hides Level 3. Figure 5-3 shows a project that has three outline levels, and all are displayed. Figure 5-4 shows the same project with only two outline levels displayed.

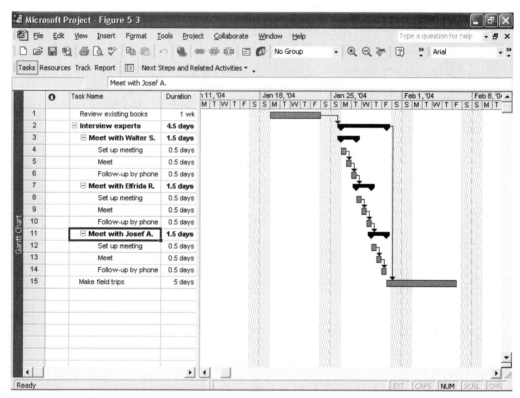

Figure 5-3 A project that has three outline levels.

Figure 5-4 A project that has three outline levels, of which only two are displayed.

NOTE *In Project, you can have as many as nine outline levels. That is, a summary task can have a maximum of eight levels of subtasks.*

Promoting and Demoting Tasks

To promote a task, you simply select it and click the Outdent toolbar button. It does not become a summary task, though, until you either insert subtasks or demote subsequent tasks. To demote a task, you select it and click the Indent toolbar button. When you demote a task or a group of tasks, you see the following changes:

- The task immediately preceding becomes a summary task and is in boldface.

- The selected tasks are indented to the right.

- A summary bar appears in the Gantt chart, as Figure 5-5 shows. In the figure, you can see three levels of summary bars.

Step 5 Review Project Organization

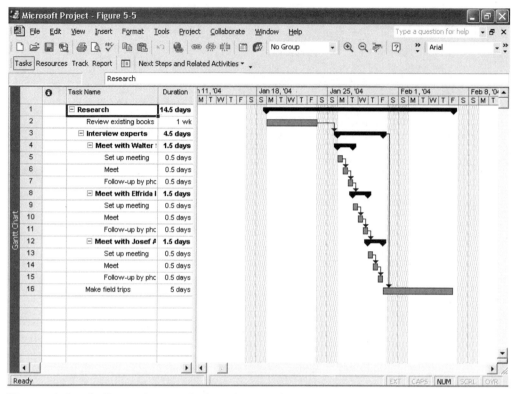

Figure 5-5 A Gantt chart with three levels of summary bars.

You can always tell which tasks have subtasks. Tasks that are above other tasks appear in boldface letters.

Editing or Deleting Summary Tasks

As you're reviewing the organization of your project, you may well find that you want to change the wording of a summary task, for example, to more accurately reflect the grouping, and you may also want to delete a summary task. To change a summary task, simply select it and edit its contents in the Entry bar.

Deleting a summary task is a bit trickier than it might seem. The problem is that whenever you delete a summary task, you also delete its associated subtasks, and that isn't necessarily what you want to do. To see how this works, take the following actions:

1. **Select a summary task in your project.**

   To select a task, click its number.

2. **Press the Delete key.**

   You'll now see the Planning Wizard dialog box, as shown in Figure 5-6. The Planning Wizard warns you that deleting a summary task also deletes its subtasks and gives you the opportunity to change your mind.

Figure 5-6 The Planning Wizard dialog box.

3. **If you want to delete both the summary task and its subtasks, click OK.**

   If you don't want to delete both kinds of tasks, click Cancel, and then click OK.

If you don't see the Planning Wizard dialog box, take the following actions:

1. **Choose the Tools menu's Options command.**

   Project displays the Options dialog box.

2. **Click the General tab.**

   Project displays the General tab of the Options dialog box.

3. **Select the Advice From Planning Wizard check box and all its subordinate check boxes.**

4. **Click OK.**

   This applies your changes and closes the Options dialog box.

   TIP   *It's a good idea to leave all the wizards enabled until you become familiar with the way Project works. When the wizards start to annoy you, you can clear the check boxes on the General tab of the Options dialog box to disable them.*

But you still need to know how to delete a summary task without deleting its subtasks, right? To do this, take the following actions:

1. **Select the subtasks.**

   To do that, hold down the Ctrl key as you click task numbers.

2. **Click the Outdent toolbar button.**

   This promotes the subtasks to the same level as the summary task.

3. **Select the summary task, and press the Delete key.**

Moving Tasks and Summary Tasks

In the process of reviewing the organization of a project, you will very likely come across a task or a summary task that needs to be moved. For example, in the off-site seminar plan mentioned earlier in this step, suppose you want the event to take place at the Executive Plaza Resort, and you've found out that its conference rooms are booked except for one week this quarter and one week the next quarter. Because the date will now be determined by the availability of the place, you need to switch steps 1 and 2.

To switch tasks 1 and 2, take the following actions:

1. **Select task 2.**

   Click the gray number 2 box at the left end of the task to select the entire row.

2. **Hold down the left mouse button, and drag the cursor up until it rests on the line above task 1.**

   As you drag, you'll see a gray line appear.

3. **Release the mouse button.**

   Task 1 and task 2 are now switched. Notice that the durations, resources, and costs travel with the task when it is moved.

To move a group of tasks, take the following actions:

1. **Select the first task in the group.**

   Click the gray box at the left end of the task to select it.

2. **Press and hold down the Shift key, and select the number of the last task in the group.**

   This selects all the tasks in between as well.

3. **Release the mouse button and the Shift key.**

4. **Click the group that you just selected, and drag until you reach the line above the row where you want to relocate the tasks.**

   As you drag, a gray line appears.

5. **Release the mouse button.**

    This drops the group of tasks in the new location.

You move summary tasks in the same way that you move any other task. Remember, however, that all of a summary task's subtasks move right along with it, as well as all associated durations, resources, and costs. Another point to be aware of when moving summary tasks is that if you move a summary task into an existing summary group, the summary task you move becomes a subtask of that group. In addition, the subtasks of the summary task that you move then become sub-subtasks.

> **TIP** *Don't forget about the Undo toolbar button when you're moving tasks around. If you move a task to the wrong place, simply click Undo to restore it to its original location.*

Collapsing and Expanding Tasks

Another helpful way to look at your project, especially if it is long and complicated, is to collapse tasks. To hide an individual summary task's subtasks, click the minus sign next to the summary task or click on the task and then click the Hide Subtasks toolbar button. To then display the subtasks, click the plus sign or click the Show Subtasks toolbar button. To display only the summary tasks in your project, take the following actions:

1. **Select the entire project by clicking the Select All button.**

    This button is the cell above the first ID number. The ID numbers are in the leftmost column of the Gantt table. After you click the button, the entire Gantt chart is highlighted.

2. **Click the Hide Subtasks button on the Formatting toolbar.**

    Project collapses to the topmost summary task. So if you have a single summary task for the entire project, Project collapses the entire project. Click Show Subtasks to show the next level of summary tasks. Click Show Subtasks as many times as necessary to display all subtasks in the project.

Adding Outline Symbols and Numbers

By default, Project inserts plus and minus signs next to summary tasks. You can remove them if you want, and you can also number your outline using the options on the View tab of the Options dialog box. To do so, take the following actions:

1. **Choose the Tools menu's Options command.**

   Project displays the Options dialog box.

2. **Click the View tab.**

   Figure 5-7 shows this tab.

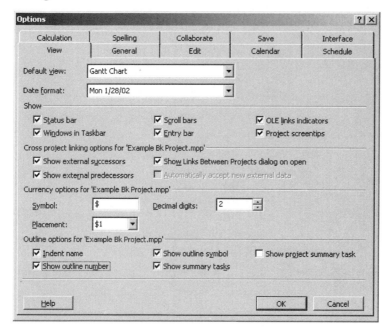

Figure 5-7   The View tab on the Options dialog box.

3. **Select the Show Outline Number check box.**

   To hide the plus and minus signs, clear the Show Outline Symbol check box as well. You will find these options near the bottom of the dialog box.

4. **Click OK.**

Table 5-1 lists and describes all the outlining options on the View tab.

NOTE   *Project uses the outlining structure that conforms to the WBS (Work Breakdown Structure) project management system, which organizes tasks to facilitate detailed reporting and tracking of costs.*

OPTION	WHAT IT DOES
Indent Name	Indents each level of subtask to the right. Clear this check box if you want to align, rather than indent, all subtasks.
Show Outline Number	Displays a number in front of all summary tasks and subtasks. Clear this check box if you don't want to use outline numbering.
Show Outline Symbol	Displays a plus/minus sign in front of each summary task. Clear this check box if you don't want to display these symbols.
Show Summary Tasks	Displays summary tasks. Clear this check box if you don't want to display summary tasks.
Show Project Summary Task	Displays the name of your project in row 0 of the Gantt table. Clear this check box if you don't want to display the project name.

Table 5-1   Outlining options in Project.

Depending on how you plan to use the information you're storing in your project, outlining can come in handy. Figure 5-8 shows a project that uses outline numbering to give a clearer picture of how tasks are subordinate to other tasks.

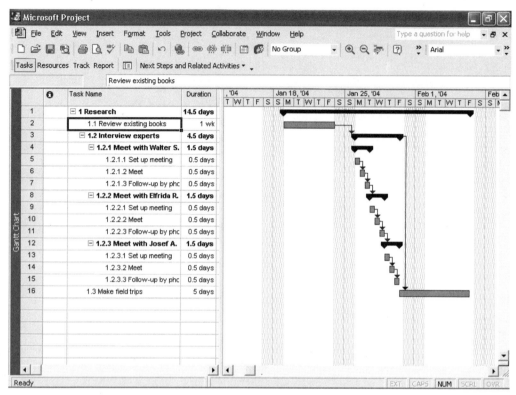

Figure 5-8   A project that uses outline numbering.

Changing the Timescale

By default, the timescale on the Gantt chart shows weeks on the top line and days on the bottom line, as shown in Figure 5-9. You can easily change the timescale to display more or less detail by clicking the Zoom In and Zoom Out toolbar buttons (or by pressing Ctrl+/ or Ctrl+*). You can zoom out all the way to half-year intervals, and you can zoom in all the way to quarter-hour intervals.

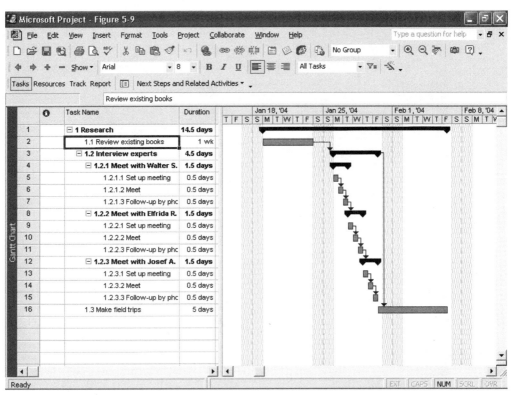

Figure 5-9 By default, the Gantt chart timescale display days and weeks.

Depending on the complexity and scope of your project, you may find it helpful to zoom out and take a look at the big picture—either on the screen or in print. ("Step 6: Present Project to Stakeholders" discusses printing.) Figure 5-10 shows the same project as in Figure 5-9, but the timescale has been zoomed out to display the months of the year, rather than the days and weeks.

Step 5 Review Project Organization

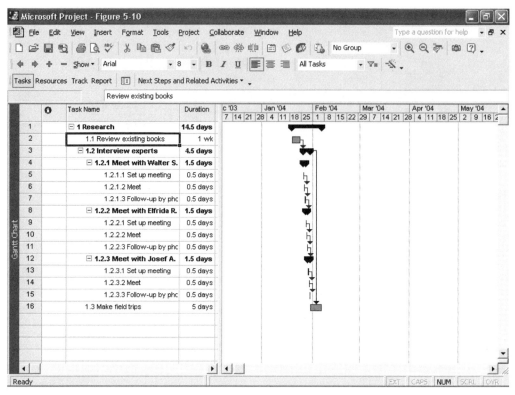

Figure 5-10 The timescale is zoomed out to show months and years.

Using Filters

Thus far, you've seen a number of ways that you can view and manipulate the information in a project, but this book has only just begun to introduce you to the myriad features at your disposal once the to-do list in your head is in electronic form. This section looks at *filters*. A filter is simply a device you can use to segregate and display only specific information. For example, suppose you want to see only the tasks that one person will perform on the current project or only tasks that are not yet complete. To get this information, you use a filter.

Project has two kinds of filters:

- Standard filters that are predefined in Project.
- Filters that you create.

Each type serves a particular purpose, and this section gives you some tips for when you might want to use each type.

The default filter is All Tasks. You can always tell which filter is active by looking at the Filter box on the Formatting toolbar, as shown in Figure 5-11.

Figure 5-11 The Filter box indicates the active filter.

TIP   *You can return to the default filter, All Tasks or All Resources, at any time by pressing F3.*

Standard Filters

Project provides 56 standard filters, and they are of two types:

- Task filters: As their names suggest, task filters let you segregate information about tasks. For example, you can find out which tasks are complete, which are not yet started, which are associated with overtime, and so on. Task filters are available when using views that are primarily task-based, such as the Calendar and Gantt chart views.
- Resource filters: Resource filters let you segregate information about resources, such as which are overallocated, which are slipping behind, and so on. Resource filters are available when using views that are primarily resource-based, such as the Resource Graph and Resource Sheet views.

Table 5-2 lists and describes the task filters, and Table 5-3 lists and describes the resource filters.

FILTER	WHAT IT SHOWS
All Tasks	All tasks in the project.
Completed Tasks	All finished tasks.
Confirmed	The tasks that resources have agreed to accept.
Cost Greater Than	The tasks that will cost more than the amount you designate.
Cost Overbudget	Tasks that will cost more than the baseline amount. This is a calculated filter.
Created After	All tasks that were created after a date you specify. This is an interactive filter.
Critical	All tasks on the critical path.
Date Range	All tasks that start or finish between two dates that you specify. This is an interactive filter.
In Progress Tasks	All tasks that have begun but are not finished.
Incomplete Tasks	All unfinished tasks.
Late/Overbudget Tasks Assigned To	Tasks associated with the resource you specify that exceed the budget or that will finish after the baseline finish date.
Linked Fields	Tasks that are linked to values in another program, such as a worksheet in Microsoft Excel.
Milestones	All tasks that are milestones.
Resource Group	Tasks associated with the resources of the group you specify. This is an interactive filter.
Should Start By	All tasks that should have started by a date you specify but have not done so. This is an interactive filter.
Should Start/Finish By	Tasks that haven't started and finished within a date range that you specify. This is an interactive filter.
Slipped/Late Progress	Tasks that are behind the scheduled finish date or that are not moving along on schedule.

FILTER	WHAT IT SHOWS
Slipping Tasks	All tasks that are running behind schedule.
Summary Tasks	All tasks that have subtasks.
Task Range	All tasks that have ID numbers within a range you specify. This is an interactive filter.
Tasks with Attachments	All tasks that have an attached object or a note.
Tasks with a Task Calendar Assigned	Tasks that have objects and a calendar associated with them.
Tasks with Deadlines	Tasks for which you set a deadline.
Tasks with Estimated Durations	Tasks for which you specified that the duration was an estimate.
Tasks with Fixed Dates	All tasks that do not have the As Soon As Possible constraint or that have an actual start date.
Tasks/Assignments with Overtime	Tasks for which resources are working overtime.
Top Level Tasks	The highest-level tasks. Use this filter if your project has summary tasks within summary tasks.
Unconfirmed	Tasks for which you have requested resources and at least one resource has declined to accept.
Unstarted Tasks	Tasks not yet begun.
Update Needed	Revised tasks that need to be sent for update or confirmation.
Using Resource in Date Range	All tasks assigned to a resource that you specify that start and finish within dates you specify. This is an interactive filter.
Using Resource	All tasks that use the resource you specify. This is an interactive filter.
Work Overbudget	All tasks with scheduled work that is more than their baseline work. This is a calculated filter.

Table 5-2   The task filters.

RESOURCE	WHAT IT SHOWS
All Resources	All the resources in a project.
Confirmed Assignments	All assignments that have been accepted by their resources. You can use this filter only in the Resource Usage view.
Cost Greater Than	All resources that will cost more than the amount you specify. This is an interactive filter.
Cost Overbudget	All resources that have a scheduled cost that is more than their baseline cost. This is a calculated filter.
Date Range	All tasks and resources that start or finish within a date range that you supply. This is an interactive filter.
Group	All resources that belong to a group you specify. This is an interactive filter.
In Progress Assignments	Assignments that are started but that are not finished. You can use this filter only in Resource Usage view.
Linked Fields	Resources to which text from another application is linked, such as Microsoft Word.
Overallocated Resources	Resources that you have assigned more work than is possible in the allotted time.
Resource Range	All resources within a range of ID numbers that you specify. This is an interactive filter.
Resources – Material	All non-human resources, such as computers, paper, calculators, and so on.
Resources with Attachments	Resource to which objects or notes are attached.
Resources/Assignments with Overtime	Resources or assignments that are working overtime.
Resources – Work	Resources such as people or equipment.
Should Start By	All tasks and resources that should start by a date that you specify but have not done so. This is an interactive filter.

RESOURCE	WHAT IT SHOWS
Should Start/Finish By	Tasks that should have started and finished within a date range you specify. This is an interactive filter.
Slipped/Late Progress	Resources whose tasks have not been finished by their baseline finish date or that are moving along on schedule.
Slipping Assignments	Resources whose tasks are not moving along according to their baseline plan and are not yet completed.
Unconfirmed Assignments	Assignments that have not been accepted by their resources.
Unstarted Assignments	Assignments that have not yet begun.
Work Complete	Resources that have finished all their assigned tasks.
Work Incomplete	Resources that have scheduled work less than their baseline work. This is a calculated filter.
Work Overbudget	Resources that have scheduled work that is more than their baseline work. This is a calculated filter.

Table 5-3   The resource filters.

In most views, you can access all the standard filters, as well as filters you create, by using the following tools:

- The Filtered For command
- The Filter box
- The More Filters command
- The AutoFilter command

Each tool gives you a distinct view of the filtered information.

As this section details the different ways that you can apply filters, you'll begin to notice that you can get the same information in various ways. For example, you can display all the tasks that one person is responsible for by using an AutoFilter or by using an interactive filter. Which method you use depends partly on the view and partly on your personal preference.

Using a filter to segregate information does just that. It does not change or remove any of the information in your project. And don't forget: to return to the default view (All Tasks) at any time, simply press F3.

NOTE *When you apply one filter and then apply a second filter, the second filter applies to the entire project, not just to the information that was displayed when you ran the first filter.*

Access Filters with the Filtered For Command

NOTE *The following section discusses task filters. The same techniques apply to resource filters.*

You use the Filtered For command to access ten commonly used filters, as well as the More Filters command:

- All Tasks
- Completed Tasks
- Critical
- Date Range
- Incomplete Tasks
- Milestones
- Summary Tasks
- Task Range
- Tasks with Estimated Durations
- Using Resource

To use the Filtered For command to display all completed tasks, choose the Project menu's Filtered For: All Tasks command and choose the submenu's Completed Tasks command. Figure 5-12 shows only the completed tasks for the book-publishing project. This type of filtered view is called an *isolated filter view*.

Figure 5-12 The book-publishing project, filtered for completed tasks.

TIP *The fastest way to apply a filter is to choose one from the Filter drop-down menu. You will find this menu on the right side of the Formatting toolbar.*

Instead of displaying only the completed tasks, you can also display the entire project and completed tasks in a different color. This type of filtered view is called a *highlighted filter view*. To do this, take the following actions:

1. **Hold down the Shift key.**
2. **Choose the Project menu's Filtered For: Completed Tasks command and choose the submenu's Completed Tasks command.**

   Project displays the completed tasks in blue.

Step 5 Review Project Organization

Access Filters with the Filter Box

As mentioned earlier, you can always tell which filter is active by looking at the Filter box on the Formatting toolbar, but you can also use the Filter box to select and apply a filter. Click the drop-down arrow, and then scroll down through the list to see the available filters. The Filter box displays the standard filters and the filters you create. (Later in this section, we'll look at how to create your own filters.)

Access Filters with the More Filters Command

You can use the More Filters command to apply other filters, but its real purpose is to allow you to select, edit, create, format, and organize filters. Earlier we looked at how to display filtered tasks in a color that is different from the color of the other tasks. By default, that color is blue, but you can change it to another color using the More Filters dialog box and the Text Styles dialog box. To do this, take the following actions:

1. Choose the Project menu's Filtered For: command, and then choose the submenu's More Filters command.

    Project displays the More Filters dialog box, as shown in Figure 5-13.

    Figure 5-13 The More Filters dialog box.

2. **Select a filter, and then click the Highlight button.**

    The filtered tasks you selected now appear in blue.

3. **Choose the Format menu's Text Styles command.**

    Project displays the Text Styles dialog box, as shown in Figure 5-14.

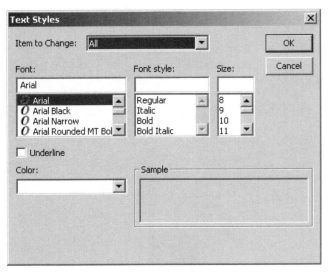

Figure 5-14 The Text Styles dialog box.

4. **Select Highlighted Tasks from the Item To Change drop-down list box.**

   TIP *This list isn't in alphabetic order, and you'll need to scroll down to about the middle to find Highlighted Tasks.*

5. **Select a color from the Color drop-down list box, and then click OK.**

   What was formerly blue is now displayed in the color you selected. You can also use the Text Styles dialog box to change the font, the font size, and emphasis (such as bold or italic).

You can, of course, use the More Filters box to simply apply a filter. To do so, select the filter and then click the Apply button. A later section looks at how to use the More Filters dialog box to create your own filter.

Using AutoFilters

An AutoFilter applies to a single column in a Gantt table. For example, you can choose the Today AutoFilter in the Finish column to display only the tasks in your project that will be completed today, as shown in Figure 5-15. By default, AutoFilters are not enabled; to turn them on, click the AutoFilter button on the Formatting toolbar. You'll then see a drop-down arrow on the right of each column heading. Figure 5-15 shows AutoFilters turned on and the drop-down menu that appears when you click the Finish AutoFilter.

Step 5 Review Project Organization   **111**

Figure 5-15 An AutoFilter in action.

To get an idea of what filters are available with AutoFilter, take a moment to click the drop-down arrow and check out the menu that appears with each column in the Gantt table.

NOTE *You cannot apply AutoFilters in the Calendar, Resource Graph, Network Diagram, or Form views.*

An important feature of AutoFilter is the Custom command, which might sound advanced but is really simple to use. Let's use it to filter out a start date. To do this, take the following actions:

1. Click the down arrow in the Start column of the Gantt table, and select Custom.

Project displays the Custom AutoFilter dialog box, as shown in Figure 5-16.

Figure 5-16   The Custom AutoFilter dialog box.

2. **Select Does Not Equal from the Start drop-down list box.**

   The items in this drop-down list are called *comparison operators*.

3. **In the drop-down box to the right, select a date.**

4. **Click OK.**

   Now all tasks associated with the start date you selected are filtered out.

Using Interactive Filters

If you perused Tables 5-2 and 5-3 earlier in this step, you noticed that some filters are described as interactive. An interactive filter requires that you specify some information, such as the name of a resource or a date range. If a filter is interactive, its name in the Filtered For: All Tasks submenu is followed by an ellipsis (...). As is the case in all Microsoft Windows programs, an ellipsis indicates that clicking the item opens a dialog box.

When you're using an interactive filter, you use its dialog box to enter information. To see how this works, let's filter for a task range. To do this, take the following actions:

1. **Choose the Project menu's Filtered For: command and choose the submenu's Task Range command.**

   Project displays the Task Range dialog box, as shown in Figure 5-17.

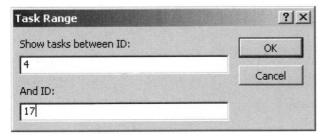

Figure 5-17   The Task Range dialog box.

2. **Specify the ID range of the tasks you want to display.**

    In the Show Tasks Between ID text box, enter the first ID of the range of tasks you want to display. In the And ID text box, enter the last ID of the range of tasks you want to display.

3. **Click OK.**

    Now you'll see only tasks that fall within the range of ID numbers you specified.

    TIP *If you want to highlight the task range rather than displaying it in isolated filter view, press and hold down the Shift key while taking actions 1 and 2.*

Managing with Filters

You should be able to use Project's filters for most of your nuts-and-bolts managing. My most common project management task, for example, was to use Project's AutoFilters on a weekly basis to check which tasks were supposed to finish in the current week and which tasks were supposed to start in the coming week. With this information in hand, I found it easy to verify either with a short e-mail message or a quick telephone call that the person responsible for a task was finishing or starting on time.

I typically performed this quick check and review on Friday mornings. The Friday-morning timing meant I could still connect and communicate with team members heading off for an early weekend or those team members working in a different time zone. And the timing meant I could (usually) start my weekend with the knowledge that the project was on track for the next week.

Creating a Filter

With all the predefined filters at your fingertips, you might find it difficult to imagine why you would ever need to define a custom filter. The time will come, however, and then you can turn back to this section of the book for details.

You can create a new filter from scratch, or you can edit an existing filter to accommodate your needs. Let's start with the latter.

Editing an Existing Filter

To create a new filter from an existing one, take the following actions:

1. **Choose the Project menu's Filtered For: command, and then choose the submenu's More Filters command.**

    Project displays the More Filters dialog box.

2. If necessary, select the Task option, and then select a filter from the list.

3. Click Copy.

   Project displays the Filter Definition dialog box, as shown in Figure 5-18.

Figure 5-18 The Filter Definition dialog box.

4. Type a name for your new filter in the Name box.

   Select the Show In Menu check box so that your new filter will appear in the Filtered For submenu. If necessary, select the Field Name and change it.

5. Specify the criteria a task must meet for Project to display or highlight it.

   Select the contents in the Test column, and click the down arrow to select a comparison operator. Select the contents in the Value(s) column, and click the down arrow to select a value.

6. Click OK.

   The name of your new filter appears in the More Filters dialog box. To apply it, click Apply.

Creating a New Filter

To create a new filter, take the following actions:

1. **Choose the Project menu's Filtered For: command, and then choose the submenu's More Filters command.**

   Project displays the More Filters dialog box.

2. **Click New.**

   Project displays the Filter Definition dialog box, empty and ready for you to use it to create a new filter, as shown in Figure 5-19.

Figure 5-19 The Filter Definition dialog box.

3. **Name the new filter.**

   Enter a name for your new filter in the Name box. The name you enter will appear in the Filter box on the Formatting toolbar.

4. **Select the Show In Menu check box.**

   When you select this option, Project lists the name of your new filter in the Filtered For menu.

5. **Specify the criteria a task must meet for Project to display or highlight it.**

   Select the Field Name box, and then click the down arrow to select a field from the list. Select the Test box, and then click the down arrow to select a comparison operator from the list. Select the Value(s) box, and then click the down arrow to select a value from the list.

6. **Click OK.**

Sorting Tasks and Resources

Yet another way to look at the information in your project is to sort it. For example, you could arrange tasks or resources in alphabetic order instead of ID number order. You may remember that when you apply a filter to a project and then apply another filter, the second filter works on the entire project, not on the display that resulted from the first filter.

When you're sorting in Project, however, you need to be aware that the sort will apply to the current view. If you filter on Summary Tasks, for example, and then run a sort, the sort applies only to Summary Tasks, which are displayed in the current view.

To see how sorting works, let's sort on Resource Names. If you have a large, complicated project, you might very well want to do this and then print your Gantt table so that all the people involved in the project can see at a glance the tasks for which they are responsible and the part of the schedule that involves them. Take the following actions:

1. **Switch to the Task Sheet view.**

   Choose the View menu's More Views command to open the More Views dialog box, select Task Sheet, and then click the Apply button.

2. **Choose the Project menu's Sort command, and then choose the submenu's Sort By command.**

   Project displays the Sort dialog box, as shown in Figure 5-20.

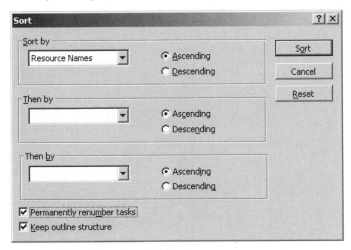

Figure 5-20 The Sort dialog box.

3. **In the Sort By box, click the down arrow and select Resource Names from the list.**

4. **Make sure that the Permanently Renumber Tasks check box is cleared.**

   If you allow Project to permanently renumber tasks when sorting, you can get some unexpected and unwanted results that can damage your task relationships. Of course, if this happens, you can always click the Undo toolbar button and sort again after you clear this check box.

5. **Leave the Keep Outline Structure check box selected.**

   By clearing the Permanently Renumber Tasks check box and leaving the Keep Outline Structure check box selected, you tell Project not reassign ID numbers. In addition, all subtasks stay with their summary tasks.

6. **Click the Sort button.**

Figure 5-21 shows a small project sorted by Resource Names.

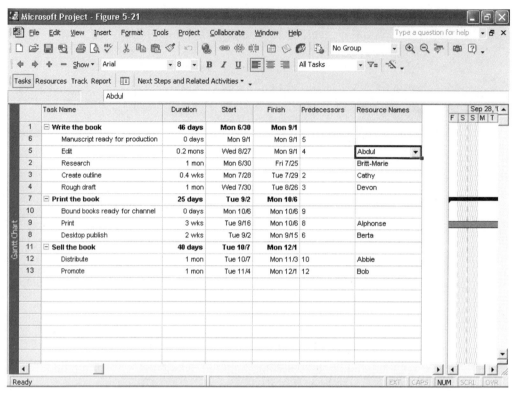

Figure 5-21 A book-publishing project sorted by Resource Names.

Looking at Your Project in Various Views

A *view* is simply a way to display the information in a project. You can look at your project in various views to focus on its different aspects. The default view, which you've seen many times in this book, is the Gantt Chart view, which is actually a table and a bar chart. In this view, you enter task information in the pane on the left, and the chart in the pane on the right displays a graphical representation of that information.

If, however, you want to zero in on a particular aspect of your project, you can display the information in a different view. For example, if you want to check out resource allocations, you'll probably want to display your project in Resource Graph view, as demonstrated in "Step 4: Identify and Allocate Resources."

> **TIP** *Gantt Chart view is the default view, but you can change that if you want. Choose the Tools menu's Options command and select the View tab. Then, on the Default View drop-down list, choose a view other than Gantt Chart.*

118 *Project 2002: Effective Project Management in Eight Steps*

Understanding the Types of Views

In Project, you can display information in three types of views:

- Chart or graph, which presents information as pictures.
- Sheet, which presents information as it might appear in a table or a worksheet.
- Form, which presents information about a single task as it might appear on a paper form.

Views can also be categorized according to whether they contain information about tasks or resources. For example, the Gantt Chart view is a task view. In Step 4, you looked at three types of resource views:

- Resource Sheet
- Resource Graph
- Resource Usage

Table 5-4 lists the available views in Project and describes the circumstance in which each is used. The following sections look at some of these views in detail, and discuss how to create a new view. To display one of the most commonly used views, choose its name on the View menu. To display any of the other default views, take the following actions:

1. Choose the View menu's More Views command.

Project displays the More Views dialog box, as shown in Figure 5-22.

Figure 5-22 The More Views dialog box.

Step 5 Review Project Organization

2. Select a view from the Views list, and then click the Apply button.

VIEW	WHAT IT SHOWS	USE IT TO
Bar Rollup	A list of summary tasks and labels for all subtasks	Display all tasks concisely labeled on summary task bars.
Calendar	A one-month calendar of tasks and durations.	Display the scheduled tasks for a range of weeks.
Descriptive Network Diagram	A graphical representation of all tasks and task dependencies.	Create and adjust your schedule in flowchart format.
Detail Gantt	Tasks, related information, and a chart.	Determine how much a task can slip without affecting other tasks.
Gantt Chart	Entry table and a chart.	Enter and schedule tasks.
Leveling Gantt	Task list, tasks delays and slack, and a bar chart that shows the effects before and after leveling.	Check for task delay.
Milestone Date Rollup	Summary tasks and labels for all subtasks.	See tasks concisely labeled and milestone marks and dates on summary task bars.
Milestone Rollup	Summary tasks that contain labels for all subtasks.	See tasks concisely labeled and milestone marks on summary task bars.
Multiple Baselines Gantt	The various baselines you saved.	Compare your original project estimates to actual plan outcomes.
Relationship Diagram	A graphical representation of the predecessors and successors or a single task.	Focus on the dependencies of a single task.
Resource Allocation	The Resource Usage view in the top pane and the Leveling Gantt view in the bottom pane.	Resolve overallocations of resources.
Resource Form	A paperlike form.	Enter and edit information about a single resource.
Resource Graph	A visual representation of resource allocation, cost, or overtime.	Display information about a single resource or a group of resources.
Resource Name	A paperlike form.	Enter and edit resource information.

VIEW	WHAT IT SHOWS	USE IT TO
Resource Sheet Form	A table of resources and related information.	Enter and edit resource information in a worksheet format.
Resource Usage	A list of resource allocation, cost, or work information over time.	Display cost or work allocation information for each resource and set resource contours.
Task Details Form	A paperlike form.	Review and edit tracking and scheduling information for a single task.
Task Entry	The Gantt Chart view in the top pane and the Task Form view in the bottom pane.	Add, edit, and review information about the task selected in the Gantt chart.
Task Form	A paperlike form.	Enter and edit information about a single task.
Task Name Form	A paperlike form.	Enter and edit the task name and other information.
Task Sheet	A table of tasks and related information.	Enter and schedule tasks in a worksheet format.
Task Usage	A task list that shows resources grouped under each task.	Determine which resources are assigned to which tasks and set resource work contours.
Tracking Gantt	A task list and related information, and a chart showing baseline and Gantt bars.	Compare the baseline schedule with the actual schedule.

Table 5-4   Available views in Project.

Before delving into some of the different view, we need to look at the different ways you can view tables that are contained in views. Not all views contain tables, but all tables are contained in views. One that you know very well by now is the entry table in the Gantt Chart view. If you open the Gantt Chart view and right-click the Select All button, you'll see a list of table views, as shown in Figure 5-23. You can select one of these table views, or you can click the More Tables command at the bottom of the shortcut menu to open the More Tables dialog box, as shown in Figure 5-24. The More Tables dialog box contains a list of all the available table views in Project. Click a table, and then click the Apply button to open a table in that view.

Figure 5-23 Right-click the Select All button to display a list of table views.

Figure 5-24 The More Tables dialog box displays a list of all the available table views.

The Views on the View Menu and View Bar

Earlier parts of this book described some of the views on the View menu. This section takes a look at those not discussed earlier. Let's begin with the Calendar view.

TIP   *Besides the View menu, Project 2002 offers another way to switch views— the View bar. To display the View bar, choose the View menu's View Bar command. By clicking an icon on the View bar, you can change views.*

Calendar View

Choose the View menu's Calendar command or click the Calendar icon on the View bar to display a screen similar to that shown in Figure 5-25.

NOTE   *The remainder of this step looks at how the book-publishing project appears in various views. Although some views may not be as practical as others, you'll get an idea of how different views can be effective when you're reviewing project organization.*

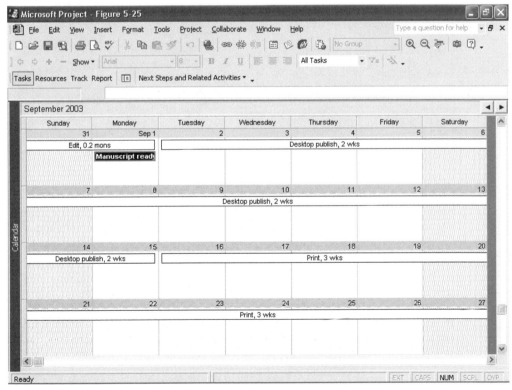

Figure 5-25 The book-publishing project in Calendar view.

Step 5 *Review Project Organization*

Before the invention of Project or any other electronic project-management tool (or even personal computers, for that matter), people used an enormous paper version of this view to track projects. People would often put a calendar and schedule on a roll of butcher paper and then tack it to the wall—all the way around the room! Maybe that's why this view looks so familiar.

In Project's Calendar view, the number of weeks you see when you first open Calendar view depends on the resolution of your monitor. On our computer, at 800-by-600 resolution, the calendar displays four weeks, as you can see in Figure 5-25. To display more or fewer weeks, take the following actions:

1. **Right-click an empty area of the calendar, and choose the shortcut menu's Zoom command.**

   Project displays the Zoom dialog box, as shown in Figure 5-26.

Figure 5-26 Use the Zoom dialog box to change the number of weeks displayed in Calendar view.

2. **Select the number of weeks you want to display and the time period, and then click OK.**

To view the previous month, click the left-pointing arrow in the upper right corner of the view. To display the next month, click the right-pointing arrow. You can also look at subsequent or previous months by dragging the slider on the vertical scroll bar.

> **TIP** Don't confuse the Calendar view with the project calendar that you use to tell Project how to handle events such as holidays and other nonworking time.

To change the information about a single task in the calendar, right-click the task and choose the shortcut menu's Task Information command to open the Task Information dialog box.

NOTE *You can, of course, print views, and the next step describes how to do so.*

Network Diagram View

If you're accustomed to working with flowcharts, you may find it effective to use the Network Diagram view. Figure 5-27 shows the book-publishing project open in Network Diagram view.

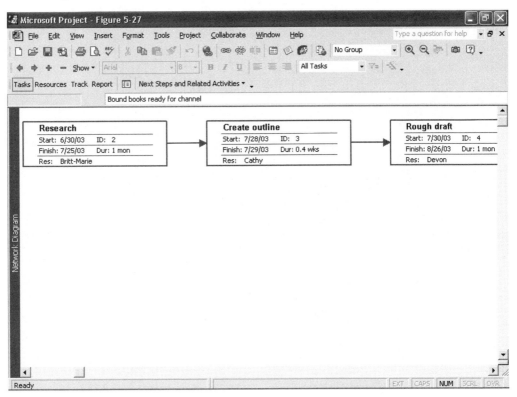

Figure 5-27 The book-publishing project open in Network Diagram view.

In this view, a box, or node, represents a task, and a line represents a dependency between tasks. A diagonal line through a task indicates that the task is in progress, and crossed diagonal lines tell you when a task is completed. To edit the information in a task box, double-click the box to open the Task Information dialog box.

If you want to adjust the position of boxes manually, choose the Format menu's Layout command to open the Layout dialog box, as shown in Figure 5-28. In this dialog box, you can also adjust the colors of the flowchart, specify whether to show summary tasks, adjust page breaks, and so on.

Figure 5-28 The Layout dialog box.

The Network Diagram view is the best view to use when you want to do any of the following:

- Link tasks and specify start and finish dates
- Display complete, in-progress, and not-yet-started tasks in graphical format
- Associate resources with specific tasks

NOTE   *Project 2002's Network Diagram view closely resembles the PERT Chart that many know from project management theory. You can accomplish many of the same tasks in Network Diagram view as you can with a PERT chart.*

Task Usage View

You use Task Usage view when you want to focus on how much work each resource has performed on a task. Figure 5-29 shows the book-publishing project in Task Usage view. The table part of this view shows task information, and the chart portion shows resource information.

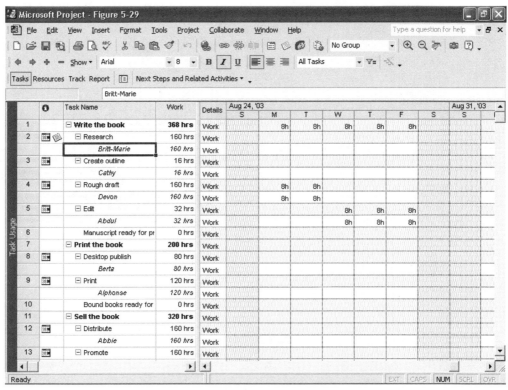

Figure 5-29 The book-publishing project in Task Usage view.

The Task Usage view is the best view to use when you want to do the following:

- Organize your resources by tasks
- Evaluate the work effort or the costs by task
- Compare the schedule with actual work performed
- Compare the planned costs with the actual costs

You can edit the entry table of this view in the same way that you edit the entry table in the Gantt Chart view.

Tracking Gantt View

Tracking Gantt view can become one of your best friends when you're tracking the progress of your project. It's a visual representation of how your project stacks up when compared with the baseline. Figure 5-30 shows the book-publishing project in Tracking Gantt view.

Figure 5-30 The book-publishing project in Tracking Gantt view.

"Step 7: Manage Project Progress" revisits this view and looks at how you update your project to track actual work and costs.

Now that you're on speaking terms with the most commonly used views, let's take a look at some of the other available views and how you can use them to review the organization of your project.

More Views

As mentioned at the beginning of this section on views, you choose the View menu's More Views command (or click the More Views icon on the View Bar) to open the More Views dialog box, which contains a list of all the views available in Project.

Let's start our tour of more views with the Detail Gantt view.

Detail Gantt View

You use Detail Gantt view to focus on slack and slippage. *Slack* is "extra time," that is, the days between the time one task ends and another starts. Technically, slack means a task can slip without delaying the project. *Slippage* may be a term you're all too familiar with. Slippage occurs when a task doesn't start on time or fails to progress according to schedule.

Figure 5-31 shows the book-publishing project in Detail Gantt view. As you can see, the only slack time for the research portion of the schedule is the weekend! It's represented by a thin line that crosses from the end of Friday to the beginning of Monday.

Figure 5-31 The book-publishing project in Detail Gantt view.

When you notice that a task is slipping, you'll probably want more detail, and so this is a good time to look at a combination view of the Detail Gantt and the Task Details form. The last section in this Step, "Displaying a Combination of Views," does just this.

Leveling Gantt View

"Step 4: Identify and Allocate Resources" discusses leveling resources, that is, resolving resource overallocation by adding resources, reducing durations, or eliminating constraints. You can view the effects of leveling resources in this view. The table portion of this view shows a list of tasks and information about delays. The chart portion shows a graphical representation of the tasks before and after leveling. Figure 5-32 shows the book-publishing project in Leveling Gantt view.

Figure 5-32 The book-publishing project in Leveling Gantt view.

To display more tasks on the timescale of the chart, click the Zoom Out toolbar button. To insert a task in the table, click the task above which you want to insert a new task, and then choose the Insert menu's New Task command.

Resource Form

This view displays information about a specific resource. First, select the name of a resource in any view, and then select the Resource Form view in the More Views dialog box. Figure 5-33 shows the Resource Form for Britt-Marie, the writer for the book-publishing project.

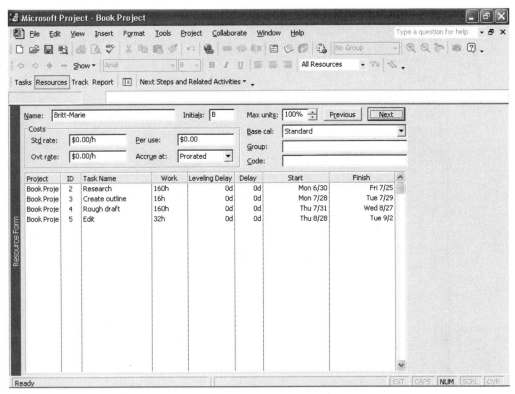

Figure 5-33 The Resource Form.

You can use this view to edit and enter information about the resource. To see other resources, click the Previous and Next buttons at the top right of this form. Unless you've sorted or filtered resources, they display in ID number order.

Resource Name Form View

This view is a stripped-down version of the Resource Form view. You can use it to view basic information about a resource. As you can do with the Resource Form, click the Previous or Next button to display this view for another resource. Figure 5-34 shows the Resource Name Form for Britt-Marie.

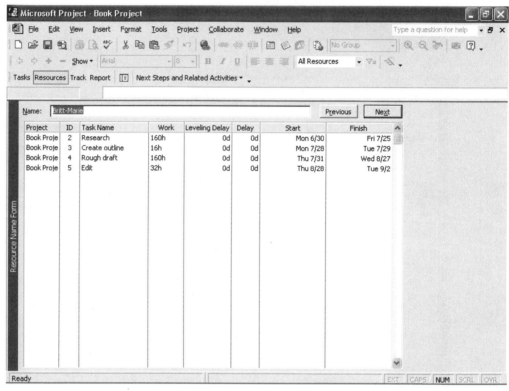

Figure 5-34 The Resource Name Form.

TIP   *If you lose a resource—perhaps a project team member leaves the project— the Resource Name Form view is a fast way to identify all the tasks you'll need to reassign.*

Task Details Form View

You use this view to display detailed information about a single task. First, select the task in any view, and then choose the Task Details Form view from the More Views dialog box. Figure 5-35 shows the Create outline task from the book-publishing project in Task Details Form view. Click the Previous or Next button to display details about another task.

Figure 5-35 The Task Details Form.

The views you use when reviewing or working on any project depend, of course, on what you want to know. You'll probably find yourself most often using the views available on the View menu, but take a little time to experiment with the other views available in the More Views dialog box so that you'll have an idea about what you might find helpful in a specific situation.

Now let's look at one more way you can view information in Project—a combination view.

Displaying a Combination of Views

As mentioned earlier in the discussion of the Detail Gantt view, you can display two views in a split window. For example, while displaying the Detail Gantt view, select a task, and choose the Window menu's Split command to display the Detail Gantt view in the top pane and a form view in the bottom pane. Figure 5-36 shows the book-publishing project in such a combination view.

Figure 5-36 This combination view shows the Task Form view in the lower pane.

To change the view in the lower pane, click in the lower pane and choose a view from the View menu.

To go back to a single view, click in the half of the screen you want to continue seeing and choose the Window menu's Remove Split command.

Creating a New View

Although Project provides dozens of views that you can work with, the time may come when you need to create a new view. When you do so, you can place it on the list of available views in the More Views dialog box or include it on the View Bar. To create a new view, take the following actions:

1. **Open the More Views dialog box, and click New.**

   Project displays the Define New View dialog box, as shown in Figure 5-37.

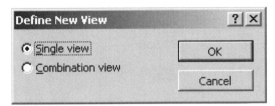

   Figure 5-37 The Define New View dialog box.

2. **Click the Single View option button, and then click OK.**

   Project displays the View Definition dialog box, as shown in Figure 5-38.

   Figure 5-38 The View Definition dialog box.

3. **Name the new view.**

   Enter a name for your new view in the Name box.

4. **Select an available view on which to base your new view.**

   Select an existing view from the Screen drop-down list box.

5. If the screen you select has a table, choose the table view from the Table drop-down list box.

6. If you want to specify a grouping, select it from the Group drop-down list box.

7. Optionally, specify a filter to apply to the view.

    If you want to apply a filter other than All Tasks, select it from the Filter drop-down list box.

8. If you want the information in your new view to display in the highlighted filter view, select the Highlight Filter check box.

    Instead of omitting tasks that do not fit the filter criteria from the view, Project displays all tasks and colors those that fit the criteria.

9. If you want the name of the new view to appear in the View Bar and on the View menu, select the Show In Menu check box.

    Otherwise, the name of the new view will appear only in the list in the More Views dialog box.

10. Click OK, and then click the Apply button.

    Project saves the new view and opens the current project in the new view.

Summary

The techniques talked about in this Step are guaranteed to help you avoid bad surprises. Outlining your project, checking the schedule with various timescales, filtering and sorting tasks and resources, and taking a look at your project in various views provide good protection against surprises that can thwart your project—if not throw it into a complete tailspin. You'll want to make these review processes part of your checklist before presenting your project to the stakeholders—the topic of Step 6.

Step 6

PRESENT PROJECT TO STAKEHOLDERS

Tasks Required to Complete the Step

- Printing views of your project
- Generating reports
- Exporting project information to other applications

As mentioned in previous steps, a stakeholder is any organization or individual that is involved in or affected by your project. Obviously, communicating with stakeholders is an important aspect of your job as project manager. Initially, you want your stakeholders to understand the scope of the project and their individual responsibilities, which can include everything from participating in the project to having ultimate financial say-so about whether the project even gets off the ground.

Once your project is underway, you need to keep stakeholders informed about its progress—the schedule, the costs, the availability of resources, and so on. Upper management may require periodic reports at specified intervals and may even dictate the nature of those reports.

Depending on the technological sophistication of your organization, you may be able to distribute project news via a company intranet, over e-mail, or by means of the Internet. "Step 8: Communicate Project Status" explains what you need to know to do this.

This Step describes printing the views discussed in "Step 5: Review Project Organization," generating and printing reports based on the information you've collected, and exporting Microsoft Project information to other applications. Don't fret if this exporting business sounds too technical for you; it's really not difficult once you get the hang of it, and it's a very common practice.

Simplifying the Deliverable

As you present your project to stakeholders for the first time, you may want to discuss the possibility of simplifying the deliverable. Especially the first time that stakeholders hear about the cost or time required for a project, people may find the idea of simplifying the deliverable acceptable. Of course, this opportunity isn't always available, but because the tactic can have striking effect, a quick discussion is warranted.

In the 1990s, I led a project team that wrote and produced a series of quick reference guides for Microsoft Press called Field Guides. Making a Field Guide cost roughly $100 a page and required about 16 weeks. These books boasted a very visual interior page design with lots of pictures and callout arrows that pointed to things in the screen shots. The pages were very attractive. In fact, the books won several awards. Unfortunately, these visual elements demanded a slow, by-hand page placement that caused the poor desktop publishers and the proofreaders to go nearly mad.

In 2001, I led a project team that created an equivalent series of quick references (Redmond Technology Press's A to Z Guides). By eliminating the callout arrows and using a simpler page design, the new books provided 50% more information to readers, cut the schedule to 4 weeks, and cut the cost to less than $10 a page. Modest simplification of the deliverable, in other words, provided huge decreases in the project cost and in the project schedule. And probably for most readers, the aesthetic loss was made up by the increase in information. Six of the first seven A to Z Guides are the bestselling quick references in their categories.

Printing Views of Your Project

In Project, you can print views, and you can print reports. If you've printed when using other Microsoft Windows applications, the process and the dialog boxes will look familiar. Printing a view can be as simple as opening a view and clicking the Print toolbar button. The cost of this simplicity is that you don't have any control over how and exactly what is printed. Your view is printed with the predefined default settings, which often is not what you want.

Before delving into how you specify your own settings, let's take a look at the Print Preview feature, which, as you may know from other Windows applications, displays your document on the screen just as it will appear on the printed page.

Using Print Preview

You can access Print Preview in four ways:

- By clicking the Print Preview toolbar button
- By clicking the Preview button in the Print dialog box
- By choosing the File menu's Print Preview command
- By clicking the Print Preview button in the Page Setup dialog box

When you select Print Preview, you display whatever view is currently open on your screen. For example, if you've applied a filter to a view or if you've sorted the items in your project in some way, that's what appears in Print Preview. Figure 6-1 shows the Gantt Chart view for the book-publishing project, and Figure 6-2 shows how the Gantt Chart view appears in Print Preview.

Figure 6-1 The book-publishing project in Gantt Chart view.

Figure 6-2 The Gantt Chart view in Print Preview.

Figure 6-3 The toolbar buttons in Print Preview.

Figure 6-3 shows the buttons on the Print Preview toolbar. Table 6-1 lists the buttons in order from left to right and explains how you use them to examine what will become your printed output in various levels of detail.

BUTTON	WHAT IT DOES
Page Left	Displays the previous page.
Page Right	Displays the next page.
Page Up	Displays the page above the current page in the printing order.
Page Down	Displays the page below the current page in the printing order.
Zoom	Displays an enlarged view of a portion of the current page.
One Page	Displays only a single page.
Multiple Pages	Displays all the pages of the current view in printing order.

BUTTON	WHAT IT DOES
Page Setup	Opens the Page Setup dialog box.
Print	Opens the Print dialog box.
Close	Closes the Print Preview window.
Help	Opens Help for Project.

Table 6-1 The buttons on the Print Preview toolbar.

Figure 6-4 shows how Project displays a multiple-page document when you click the Multiple Pages button. Remember that you can always click the Zoom button and then click on a page to examine it closely before you print it.

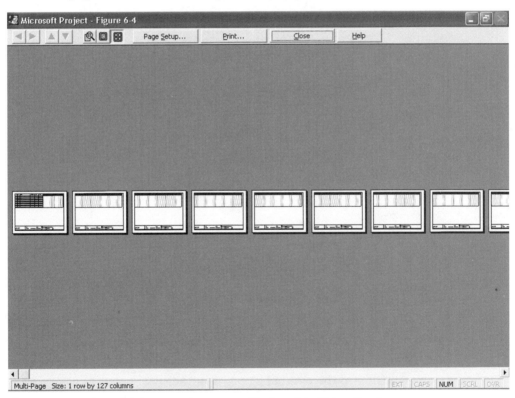

Figure 6-4 A multiple-page document displayed in Print Preview.

Understanding the Page Setup Dialog Box

To exert control over what is printed and how, you use the Page Setup dialog box, which you can open in the following ways:

- By choosing the File menu's Page Setup command
- By clicking the Page Setup button in the Print Preview window

The Page Tab

When you first open the Page Setup dialog box, it displays the Page tab, as shown in Figure 6-5. You use the options on this tab to adjust the paper orientation and the scaling and to specify the paper size and the first page number.

Figure 6-5   The Page tab of the Page Setup dialog box.

In the Orientation section of the Page tab, specify whether you want to print vertically on the page (choose Portrait) or horizontally (choose Landscape).

In the Scaling section, you can specify a percentage of the normal size in which a page would print, and you can click the Fit To button and specify that the document print on only the number of pages you specify. Obviously, the degree to which this is successful depends on the number of pages in the view you want to print.

In the Other section, you can specify a paper size. The default paper size is the one you set up in Windows, but you can specify any of the following that are allowed by your printer:

- Letter (8.5 x 11 in.)
- A4 (210 x 297 mm)
- Legal (8.5 x 14 in.)
- Executive (7.25 x 10.5 in.)
- No. 10 Envelope (4.12 x 9.5 in.)

If you want text other than "Page 1" to print on the first page, enter that in the First Page Number box.

Click the Options button to open a dialog box in which you can specify settings for your particular printer. These may include print quality, color, and so on. You'll find the Options button as well as the Print Preview button and the Print button on each tab in the Page Setup dialog box.

The Margins Tab

You use the options on the Margins tab, which is shown in Figure 6-6, to set left, right, top, and bottom margins and to specify whether you want margins around pages. The default is to print a border around every page. Figure 6-7 shows a page with a surrounding border.

Figure 6-6 The Margins tab of the Page Setup dialog box.

ID	Task Name	Duration	Start	Finish	Predecessors	Resource Names
1	**Write the book**	**40 days**	**Mon 2/14/00**	**Fri 4/7/00**		
2	Research the book's contents	1 wk	Mon 2/14/00	Fri 2/18/00		George
3	Create an outline	1 wk	Mon 2/21/00	Fri 2/25/00	2	George
4	**Write the chapters**	**30 days**	**Mon 2/28/00**	**Fri 4/7/00**	3	
5	Chapter 1	1 wk	Mon 2/28/00	Fri 3/3/00		George
6	Chapter 2	1 wk	Mon 3/6/00	Fri 3/10/00	5	George
7	Chapter 3	1 wk	Mon 3/13/00	Fri 3/17/00	6	George
8	Chapter 4	1 wk	Mon 3/20/00	Fri 3/24/00	7	George
9	Chapter 5	1 wk	Mon 3/27/00	Fri 3/31/00	8	George
10	Chapter 6	1 wk	Mon 4/3/00	Fri 4/7/00	9	George
11	**Edit the book**	**35 days**	**Mon 4/10/00**	**Fri 5/26/00**		
12	Initial edit	4 wks	Mon 4/10/00	Fri 5/5/00	10	Martha
13	Author reviews edits	1 wk	Mon 5/8/00	Fri 5/12/00	12	George
14	Final cleanup	2 wks	Mon 5/15/00	Fri 5/26/00	13	Martha
15	**Print the book**	**20 days**	**Mon 5/29/00**	**Fri 6/23/00**		
16	Prepare the files for desktop publishing	1 wk	Mon 5/29/00	Fri 6/2/00		Ben
17	Print the book	3 wks	Mon 6/5/00	Fri 6/23/00	16	Ben
18	**Sell the book**	**30 days**	**Mon 6/26/00**	**Fri 8/4/00**		
19	Distribute the book to retailers	2 wks	Mon 6/26/00	Fri 7/7/00	17	ABC Distributors
20	Promote the book to potential readers	4 wks	Mon 7/10/00	Fri 8/4/00	19	Ace Marketing Associates

Page 1

Figure 6-7 By default, Project prints a border around the edges of every page.

The Header Tab

A header is information that will appear at the top of every printed page in your document. You specify what you want in the header by selecting options on the Header tab, which is shown in Figure 6-8.

Figure 6-8 The Header tab of the Page Setup dialog box.

You use the buttons on this tab, which are listed in order from left to right in Table 6-2, to insert and format text that you specify in the Selection box. The Sample box shows how the text will appear in the header on the printed page.

BUTTON	WHAT IT DOES
Format Text Font	Opens the Font dialog box so that you can format selected text.
Insert Page Number	Prints a page number in the header.
Insert Total Page Count	Prints the total number of pages in the document.
Insert Current Date	Prints the current date in the header.
Insert Current Time	Prints the current time in the header.
Insert File Time	Prints the filename in the header.
Insert Picture	Opens the Insert Picture dialog box, from which you can select a graphic to include in the header, for example, a logo.

Table 6-2 The buttons on the Header tab.

Depending on the information stored in your project, you can also select other items to print in the header using the General and the Project Fields drop-down list boxes. Select an item, and then click Add.

After you specify the information for the header, click the Format Text Font button to open the Font dialog box, as shown in Figure 6-9. Specify the font, the font style, the font size and color, and whether you want text underlined, and then click OK to apply your choices to the selected text.

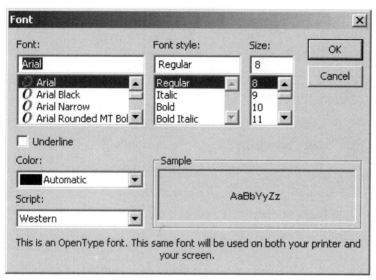

Figure 6-9   The Font dialog box.

The Footer Tab

The Footer tab, which is shown in Figure 6-10, is identical to the Header tab; however, you use the options to select information to display at the bottom of every page rather than at the top. By default, Project prints the word *Page* and the page number in the footer. If you don't want this information in the footer, select it from the Selection box, and press the Delete key.

Figure 6-10 The Footer tab of the Page Setup dialog box.

The Legend Tab

The legend describes what the bars and symbols in a chart mean. By default, a printed view contains the following in the legend at the bottom of every page, as well as the name of the project and the current date. Figure 6-11 shows the Legend tab.

- Task
- Split
- Progress
- Milestone
- Summary
- Project Summary
- External Tasks
- External Milestone
- Deadline

Figure 6-11 The Legend tab of the Page Setup dialog box.

Use the Legend tab to specify whether the legend appears on every page, only on a legend page, or not at all. You can also specify the width of the text portion of the legend in inches, and you can format the text for the legend. To format the text, click the Legend Labels button to open the Font dialog box.

You specify additional text to print in the legend using the same methods as in the Header tab and the Footer tab.

NOTE *The Legend tab is available only when you are printing in Calendar view, Gantt Chart view, or Network Diagram view.*

The View Tab

You use the View tab, as shown in Figure 6-12, to specify whether to print all or some columns, notes, and blank pages and whether to fit the timescale to the end of a page.

Figure 6-12 The View tab of the Page Setup dialog box.

After you specify all your options in the Page Setup dialog box, you can click OK, or you can click the Print button. Clicking OK displays the current view. Clicking Print opens the Print dialog box.

The Print Dialog Box

You can open the Print dialog box in the following ways:

- By choosing the File menu's Print command
- By clicking the Print button in the Print Preview windows
- By clicking the Print button in the Page Setup dialog box

Regardless of how you open it, the Print dialog box, which is shown in Figure 6-13, will look familiar if you've worked with other Windows applications.

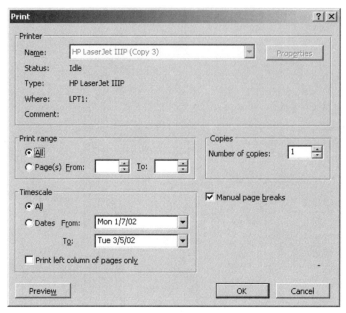

Figure 6-13 The Print dialog box.

If you want to use a printer other than the default, select it in the Name box. To change the settings for your printer, click the Properties button to open the Properties dialog box.

To select what to print, click an option button in the Print Range section. You can print all the pages or only those in the range you specify. Specify the number of copies to print in the Number Of Copies drop-down list box.

NOTE *In Project, you can't print only a selection, for example, rows 4 through 6.*

In the Timescale section, you can select to print the entire timescale or only a portion within the dates you specify. If you don't want to print the timescale, select the Print Left Column Of Pages Only check box. If you want to break between printed pages at the places you specified, select the Manual Page Breaks check box. If this check box is not checked, Project uses its automatic page breaks.

When the settings are to your liking, click OK to print your document.

TIP *To insert manual page breaks in a printed view, place the cursor where you want the break and then choose the Insert menu's Page Break command.*

Generating Reports

Although by this time you may have fallen in love with the Network Diagram view or with the Gantt Chart view of your project, printed output of either of these views may make no sense at all to a stakeholder who is not familiar with Project. Your best bet, in this case, is to distribute a standard report that looks similar to what you see in Figure 6-14.

ID	Task Name	Duration	Start	Finish
1	Publish EXEC GT FrontPage (p	111 days	Mon 10/16/00	Wed 3/21/01
17	Publish EXEC GT Access (print	103 days	Mon 11/6/00	Fri 3/30/01
33	Publish EXEC GT Word (print 2	101 days	Mon 11/13/00	Wed 4/4/01
49	Publish EXEC GT Office (print :	112 days	Mon 11/6/00	Thu 4/12/01
65	Publish EXEC GT Outlook 3/7 p	115 days	Mon 11/20/00	Tue 5/1/01
81	Publish EXEC GT PowerPoint (	88 days	Mon 11/13/00	Fri 3/16/01
97	Publish EXEC GT Excel (print 1	101 days	Mon 10/30/00	Wed 3/21/01
113	Publish MBA GT Excel (print 1/	124 days	Mon 10/2/00	Mon 3/26/01
129	Seniors Guide to Personal Con	92 days	Mon 11/13/00	Thu 3/22/01
154	Publish MBA GT Office 2/21 pri	80 days	Tue 12/26/00	Tue 4/17/01
170	Publish MBA GT WinXP (4/26)	111 days	Mon 4/16/01	Mon 9/17/01
186	Publish Exec GT WinXP (5/11)	78 days	Mon 5/28/01	Wed 9/12/01
202	Publish Exec GT Dreamweaver	62 days	Mon 11/27/00	Thu 2/22/01
218	Word From A to Z	60 days	Mon 3/5/01	Fri 5/25/01
227	Excel From A to Z	60 days	Mon 3/19/01	Fri 6/8/01
236	PowerPoint From A to Z	60 days	Mon 4/16/01	Fri 7/6/01
245	Outlook From A to Z	60 days	Mon 4/30/01	Fri 7/20/01
254	Access From A to Z	60 days	Mon 5/14/01	Fri 8/3/01

Figure 6-14 In Project, you can create a number of standard reports similar to this one.

Table 6-3 lists and describes the predefined reports you can create in Project. Later in this section, you'll see how to create a customized report.

CATEGORY	TYPE	WHAT IT SHOWS
Overview	Project Summary	Top-level information about your projects, including dates, duration, work, costs, task status, and resource status.
	Top-Level Tasks	The highest-level summary tasks as of the current date.
	Critical Tasks	The status of tasks on the critical path.
	Milestones	Information, such as planned duration, start and finish dates, predecessors, and resources, about each milestone.
	Working Days	The base calendar information.
Current Activities	Unstarted Tasks	The tasks that have not yet begun, sorted by start date.
	Tasks Starting Soon	Tasks starting within a date range that you supply.
	Tasks in Progress	Tasks that have started but that are not finished.
	Completed Tasks	All finished tasks, including the actual duration and the actual start and finish dates.
	Should Have Started Tasks	Tasks that should have begun by a date that you specify.
	Slipping Tasks	Tasks that have started which are behind schedule.
Costs	Cash Flow	The costs for weekly time increments by task.
	Budget	All tasks, the budgeted costs, and the variance between budgeted and actual cost.
	Overbudget Tasks	Cost, baseline, variance, and actual information about tasks that exceed budget
	Overbudget Resources	Resources whose cost will exceed budget based on current progress.
	Earned Value	The status of each task's cost when you compare planned to actual cost.
Assignments	Who Does What	Resources and their associated tasks, amount of work planned for each task, planned start and finish dates, and resource notes (if any).

CATEGORY	TYPE	WHAT IT SHOWS
	Who Does What When	Daily work scheduled for each resource on each task.
	To-Do List	The tasks assigned to a resource you select (on a weekly basis).
	Overallocated Resources	The overallocated resources, their tasks, and total hours of work assigned to them.
Workload	Task Usage	Tasks and their assigned resources and the amount of work assigned to each resource (in weekly increments).
	Resource Usage	Resources and the tasks assigned to them and the amount of work assigned to each resource (in weekly increments).

Table 6-3   The types of standard reports in Project.

Using the Reports Dialog Box

To generate a predefined report, take the following actions:

1. Choose the View menu's Reports command.

Project displays the Reports dialog box, as shown in Figure 6-15.

Figure 6-15   The Reports dialog box.

2. Click a report category, and then click the Select button.

Project displays the Reports dialog box for that category. Figure 6-16 shows the Reports dialog box for the Overview category.

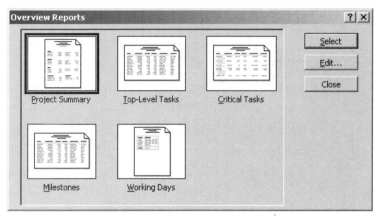

Figure 6-16 The Overview Reports dialog box.

3. Select a report type, and click the Select button.

Project displays the report in Print Preview. Figure 6-17 shows a Project Summary report open in Print Preview.

Figure 6-17 The Project Summary report open in Print Preview.

4. To print the report, click the Print button.

   Project displays the Print dialog box.

5. Specify whether you want to print all or only selected pages and the number of copies.

   Click OK when you're finished.

Understanding the Types of Reports

Table 6-3, earlier in this step, summarizes the categories of reports and the types each contains, as well as gives you an idea of the focus of each report. This section shows you what some sample reports look like.

The Overview Category

Figure 6-18 shows a Critical Tasks report for the book-publishing project.

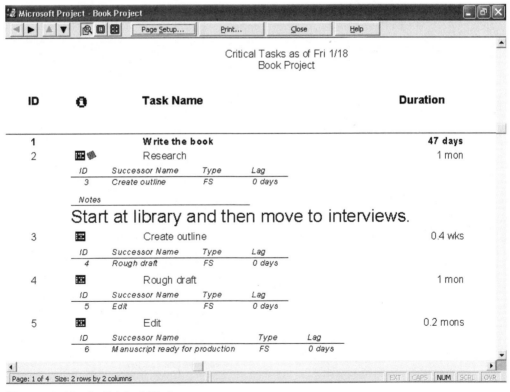

Figure 6-18 A Critical Tasks report.

Current Activities

As you can see from Table 6-3, you can specify dates for the Tasks Starting Soon report and the Should Have Started report in this category. Figure 6-19 shows the Tasks Starting Soon report for the book-publishing project.

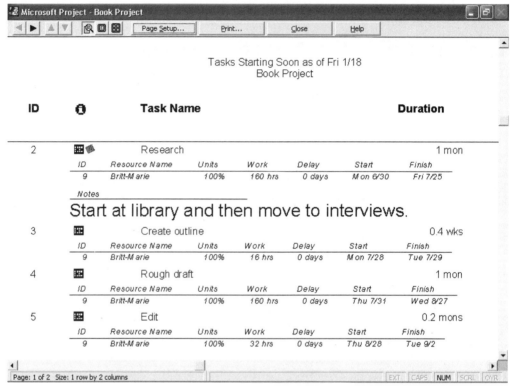

Figure 6-19 A Tasks Starting Soon report.

To create a Tasks Starting Soon report, take the following actions:

1. **Choose the View menu's Reports command.**

   Project displays the Reports dialog box.

2. **Click Current Activities, and click the Select button.**

   Project displays the Current Activity Reports dialog box, as shown in Figure 6-20.

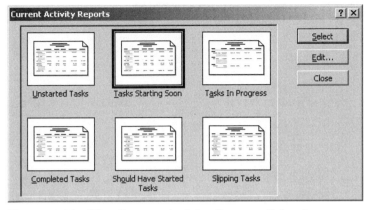

Figure 6-20 The Current Activity Reports dialog box.

3. Click Tasks Starting Soon, and click the Select button.

   Project displays the first Date Range dialog box, as shown in Figure 6-21.

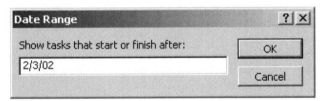

Figure 6-21 The Date Range dialog box.

4. Enter a date for which you want to show tasks that start or finish after.

5. Enter a start or a finish date, and click OK.

   Project displays a second Date Range box.

6. Enter a date that you want tasks to finish before, and click OK.

   Your Tasks Starting Soon report opens in Print Preview.

Assignments

Especially if you have a long, complex project, you might want to print out a to-do list for each project participant. Figure 6-22 shows such a list for three employees working on a book-publishing project.

Figure 6-22 A To-Do List report.

To generate the To-Do List reports, take the following actions:

1. **Open the Project file.**
2. **Choose the View menu's Reports command.**

   Project displays the Reports dialog box.

3. **Click Assignments, and then click the Select button.**

   Project displays the Assignment Reports dialog box, as shown in Figure 6-23.

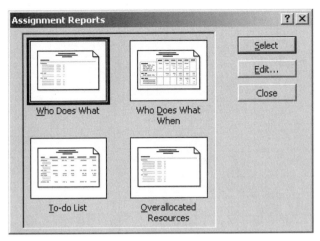

Figure 6-23 The Assignment Reports dialog box.

4. **Click To-Do List, and click the Select button.**

   Project displays the Using Resource dialog box, as shown in Figure 6-24.

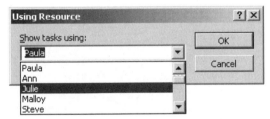

Figure 6-24 The Using Resource dialog box.

5. **Click the down arrow, select a resource, and then click OK.**

   Your To-Do List report opens in Print Preview.

Customizing a Report

As you can see from the preceding examples, the reports in Project are nicely arranged and formatted, but you can also customize a report's appearance. To do so, take the following actions:

1. **Choose the View menu's Reports command.**

   Project displays the Reports dialog box.

2. **Click Custom, and then click the Select button.**

   Project displays the Custom Reports dialog box, as shown in Figure 6-25.

Step 6 Present Project to Stakeholders

Figure 6-25 The Custom Reports dialog box.

3. **Select a report from the Reports list, and then click the Edit button.**

   For the Project Summary and Base Calendar reports, Project displays the Report Text dialog box, as shown in Figure 6-26. Select an item in the Item To Change list. Choose a font, a font style, a font size and color, and specify whether you want the item underlined, and then click OK.

   For all other reports, Project displays the Report dialog box for that type. On the Definition tab, you can rename the report, select a different time period, or change the report's table or filter. On the Details tab, you can specify the information you want to include in your report. On the Sort tab, you can select the sort order for the report.

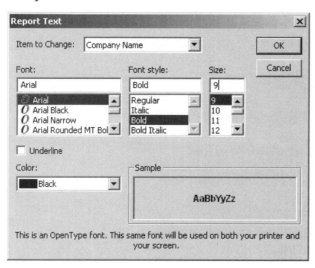

Figure 6-26 The Report Text dialog box.

4. **In the Custom Reports dialog box, click the Print button to print the report or click the Preview button if you want to check your formatting before printing.**

For some reports, all you can change is the formatting, but for other reports you can change the table, the task, or the resource filter to create a new type of report.

Creating a Report from an Existing Report

To create a report from an existing report, take the following actions:

1. **Choose the View menu's Reports command.**

   Project displays the Reports dialog box.

2. **Click Custom, and then click the Select button.**

   Project displays the Custom Reports dialog box.

3. **Select a report from the Reports list, and then click the New button.**

   Project displays the Define New Report dialog box, as shown in Figure 6-27.

Figure 6-27   The Define New Report dialog box.

4. **Select a type from the Report Type list, and click OK.**

   Project displays the Report dialog box for that type. Figure 6-28 shows the Report dialog box for the Task type.

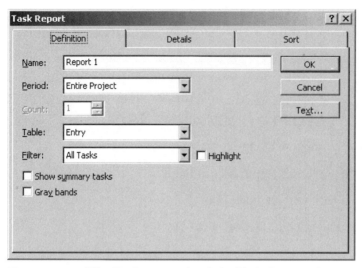

Figure 6-28 The Definition tab of the Task Report dialog box.

5. On the Definition tab, give the report a name, select a time period, and change the report's table or filter.

6. On the Details tab, select check boxes to specify the information you want to include in your report.

   Figure 6-29 shows this tab.

Figure 6-29 The Details tab of the Task Report dialog box.

7. On the Sort tab, select the sort order for the report.

   Figure 6-30 shows this tab.

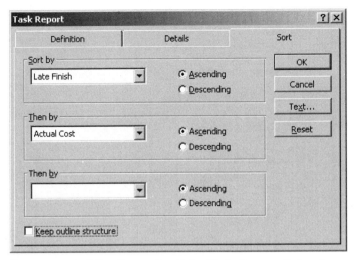

Figure 6-30 The Sort tab of the Task Report dialog box.

8. **If you want to reformat any items, click the Text button.**

   Project displays the Text Styles dialog box where you can reformat items. When you're finished, click OK.

9. **Click OK again on the Sort tab, and then click the Print button in the Custom Reports dialog box.**

   Project prints your newly created report.

Exporting Project Information to Other Applications

When you export Project information, you save it in a format that another application can read and use. For example, you might want to save cost information as a Microsoft Excel worksheet so that someone could work with it in that format. Project offers a special wizard, the Export Wizard, for saving Project data in a format that other applications can use. This section looks at how to export Project information to Excel, Microsoft Access, and HTML using one of the predefined *export maps*. You use an export map to define the information you want to export and to describe how to associate the information in the Project file with information in the other application's file.

Next, we'll look at how you can create a new export map, and then we'll describe how to export Project information to a Microsoft Word file using the Copy and Paste commands and how to create a graphic image from Project information.

Exporting to Excel

To export Project information to Excel, take the following actions:

1. **In Project, open the file that you want to export.**
2. **Choose the File menu's Save As command.**

   Project displays the Save As dialog box, as shown in Figure 6-31.

Figure 6-31 The Save As dialog box.

3. **Select a folder in which to save the file.**

   Either accept the filename that Project proposes or type a new filename in the File Name box.

4. **Select Microsoft Excel Workbook (*.xls) from the Save As Type drop-down list box, and then click the Save button.**

   Project displays the Export Wizard dialog box. The wizard will ask you a series of questions about how to save the file for use in Excel. Click the Next button.

   NOTE *You can also save the file as an Excel PivotTable, which creates two worksheets—one for the data and one for the PivotTable.*

5. **Select an option button to choose whether you want to save the file as a template or a worksheet, and click the Next button.**

   Probably you want to save the data in a worksheet. A template is a special kind of file for creating other files.

6. **Click an option button to create a new map or use an existing map, and then click the Next button.**

   Later in this Step, "Creating a New Export Map" explains what to do if you want to create an export map of your own. Export maps are blueprints for exporting data. If you click the Use Existing Map option button, you see the Map Selection dialog box shown in Figure 6-32. The names of maps you created yourself appear on this list along with maps that Project provides.

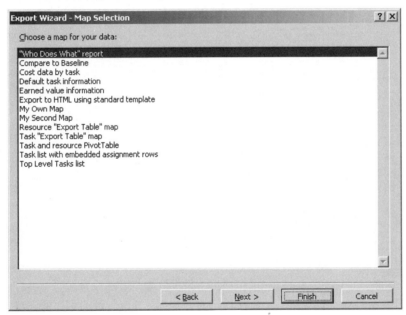

Figure 6-32 The Map Selection dialog box.

7. **Select a map from the list and click the Finish button.**

   Figure 6-33 shows the book-publishing project in Gantt Chart view in Project, and Figure 6-34 shows the task information as it appears when exported to an Excel worksheet.

Figure 6-33 The book-publishing project in Gantt Chart view.

	A	B	C	D	E	F
1	ID	Task_Name	Duration	Start_Date	Finish_Date	Predecessors
2	1	Write the book	42 days	1/7/2002 8:00	3/5/2002 17:00	
3	2	Research	1 mon	1/7/2002 8:00	2/1/2002 17:00	
4	3	Create outline	1 wk	1/30/2002 8:00	2/5/2002 17:00	
5	4	Rough draft	1 mon	2/6/2002 8:00	3/5/2002 17:00	3
6	5	Edit	1 mon	1/7/2002 8:00	2/1/2002 17:00	
7	6	Print the book	15 days	1/7/2002 8:00	1/25/2002 17:00	
8	7	Desktop publish	2 wks	1/7/2002 8:00	1/18/2002 17:00	
9	8	Shipping party	0 days	1/18/2002 17:00	1/18/2002 17:00	7
10	9	Book party	0 days	1/25/2002 17:00	1/25/2002 17:00	10
11	10	Print	3 wks	1/7/2002 8:00	1/25/2002 17:00	
12	11	Sell the book	31 days	1/7/2002 8:00	2/18/2002 17:00	
13	12	Distribute	1 mon	1/7/2002 8:00	2/1/2002 17:00	
14	13	Promote	1 mon	1/21/2002 8:00	2/18/2002 17:00	

Figure 6-34 Task information about the book-publishing project open in Excel.

Exporting to Access

To export Project information to Access, take the following actions:

1. **In Project, open the file you want to export.**
2. **Choose the File menu's Save As command.**

   Project displays the Save As dialog box.

3. **Select a folder in which to save the file.**

   Either accept the filename that Project proposes or type a new filename in the File Name box.

4. **Select Microsoft Access Databases (*.mdb) from the Save As Type drop-down list box, and then click the Save button.**

   You see the Export Wizard dialog box. From here, you will describe the data you want to export to Excel. Click the Next button.

5. **To export all the data in your project, click the A Full Project option button, click the Next button, enter a project name in the following dialog box, and click the Finish button.**

   However, you can also tell Project to export a portion of the data. Keep reading if you want to do that.

6. **To export only selected data, click the Only Selective Data option, and then click Next.**

7. **Click an option button to create a new map or use an existing map, and then click the Next button.**

   Export maps are tailor-made blueprints for exporting data. Later in this Step, "Creating a New Export Map" explains how to create a new map. If you click the Use Existing Map option button, you see the Map Selection dialog box, which lists export maps as well as the maps you create yourself.

8. **Select the items you want to export—Tasks, Resources, and/or Assignments—and then click the Finish button.**

   Project exports the data you specified to the new Access file.

Exporting to HTML

You can save a Project file as a Web page that can then be opened in a browser such as Internet Explorer. Take the following actions:

1. **Open the file that you want to save as a Web page.**
2. **Choose the File menu's Save As Web Page command.**

   Project opens the Save As dialog box, and selects the Web Page (*.html; *.htm) file type.

3. **Click the Save button.**

   Project displays the Export Wizard dialog box. Click the Next button in this dialog box.

4. **Select the Use Existing Map option button, and then click Next.**

   The next section explains what to do if you want to create a new map for exporting to another program.

5. **In the Map Selection list, choose which kind of data you want to present on the Web page, and then click the Finish button.**

   Figure 6-35 shows the book-publishing project open in Microsoft Internet Explorer. Choose the View menu's Source command to see the HTML for the file.

Figure 6-35 Project information saved as an HTML file and open in Internet Explorer.

Creating a New Export Map

If none of the existing export maps suit your needs, you can create a new one. In the following example, we'll create a new export map for a file to be exported into Excel, but the steps are essentially the same regardless of the application to which you want to export. You would simply see options specific to that program.

To create a new export map, take the following actions:

1. **In Project, open the file you want to export.**
2. **Choose the File menu's Save As command.**

   Project displays the Save As dialog box.

3. **Select a folder in which to save the file.**

   Either accept the filename that Project proposes or type a new filename in the File Name box.

4. **Select Microsoft Excel Workbook (*.xls) from the Save As Type drop-down list box, and then click the Save button.**

   Project displays the first Export Wizard dialog box. Click Next in this dialog box.

5. **Choose the Selected Data option button, and click the Next button.**
6. **Choose the New Map option button, and then click Next.**

   Project displays the Map Options dialog box, as shown in Figure 6-36.

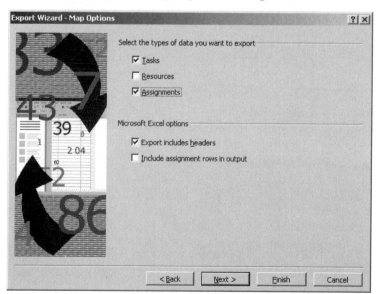

Figure 6-36 The Map Options dialog box.

170   *Project 2002: Effective Project Management in Eight Steps*

7. Select the type of data you want to import, whether you want to include page headers, and whether to include assignment rows, and then click the Next button.

   Figure 6-37 shows the Task Mapping dialog box, which appears if you choose to export tasks. If you choose to export resources and assignments as well, you also negotiate the Resources Mapping and Assignments Mapping dialog boxes.

Figure 6-37 The Task Mapping dialog box.

8. In the Destination Worksheet Name box, accept the name that Project suggests or type another one.
9. In the Export Filter drop-down list box, select the task that you want to export.
10. To add fields one at a time, click under From: Microsoft Project Field and choose a field name from the drop-down menu.

    Select the fields you want to add individually from the drop-down list.
11. Click in the To: Excel Field column in the next cell.

    Project suggests a field name, but you can change it if you want.

    As you add fields, the Preview box shows you how they will display in Excel.

    NOTE *To add all the fields in the Project file at once, click the Add All button. To clear all the fields and start over, click the Clear All button. To insert or delete a row, click the appropriate button.*

12. If you want to base your map on a table, click the Base On Table button.

    Project displays the Select Base Table For Field Mapping dialog box, as shown in Figure 6-38.

Figure 6-38 The Select Base Table For Field Mapping dialog box.

13. Select a table from the Task Tables list, and click OK.
14. When you've finished mapping fields, click the Next button.

    We can only assume that you want to save your export map, seeing as you went to all the trouble to create it.

15. Click the Save Map button, enter a name in the Save Map dialog box, and click the Save button.

    The name you enter will appear in the map list so you can choose it in the future.

16. To export the file, click the Save button.

    Click the Finish button.

Sending to Word

You can't export Project information to Word, but you can select information and then copy it to a Word document. To do so, take the following actions:

1. In Project, open the file that contains the information you want to copy.
2. Select the information, and press Ctrl+C.

    This copies the information to the Clipboard.

3. **Open the Word document, and position the cursor where you want to copy the information.**

   To paste the Project data into a blank Word document, create a new document by clicking the New toolbar button.

4. **Press Ctrl+V.**

Figure 6-39 shows the Entry table for the book-publishing project in Gantt Chart view. Figure 6-40 shows how the Task Name, Duration, Start, and Finish columns appear when copied into Word. In Word, you can convert the tab-separated columns to a table (the following Tip explains how).

Figure 6-39 The Entry table for the book-publishing project in Gantt Chart view in Project.

Step 6   Present Project to Stakeholders

Figure 6-40 The Project information after it has been copied into Word.

TIP *Unfortunately, the data is copied into Word in tab-delimited format. To turn the data into a table, select it, choose the Table menu's Convert command, and choose Text To Table on the submenu. In the Convert Text To Table dialog box that appears, make sure the Tabs option button is selected. Then click OK. The data will appear in table format, not tab-delimited format.*

Copying Project Information to a Graphics File

In addition to all the other neat ways that you can manipulate your Project information, you can copy it to a graphics file that can be displayed on a computer screen or that can be printed, and you can save the graphics file as a Graphics Interchange File (GIF) that you can open and change in an image-editing program such as Microsoft Paint. To do this, take the following actions:

1. **Open the file, and select the view of which you want a picture.**

   If you want to copy only a portion of the current display, select that portion.

2. **Click the Copy Picture toolbar button.**

   The Copy Picture button looks like a little camera. You will find it near the end of the Standard toolbar. Project displays the Copy Picture dialog box, as shown in Figure 6-41.

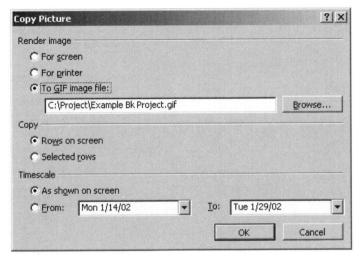

   Figure 6-41 The Copy Picture dialog box.

3. **In the Render Image section, select the type of image you want.**

   NOTE *If you selected rows before you opened the Copy Picture dialog box, click the Selected Rows option button.*

4. **Specify the range of dates over which you want the data included in the image.**

   To copy information for a range of dates other than what is currently displayed, enter the dates in the From and To boxes.

5. **Click OK to save your Project information as a picture.**

   Figure 6-42 shows a GIF image created from information in the book-publishing project and open in Paint.

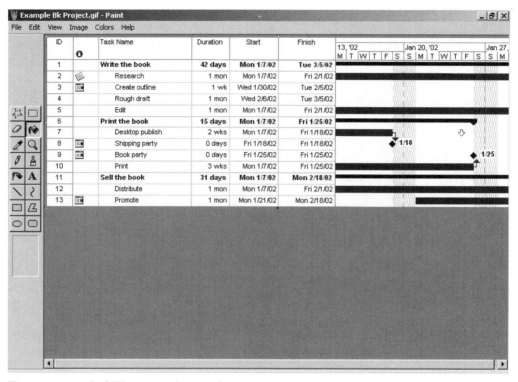

Figure 6-42 A GIF image of part of a project open in Paint.

Summary

In this Step, you've been introduced to three ways that you can present Project information to stakeholders: (1) by distributing printed views; (2) by generating and printing reports; and (3) by exporting Project information into other applications so that stakeholders can access it there. If you're in the beginning stage of a project, the next step in the process may be to get approval for your project. Once you do so, you're off and running, and the next step is to monitor the project—its schedule and costs and how what is actually being done compares with your plan. "Step 7: Manage Project Progress" shows you how to update your project to reflect what's actually taking place.

Step 7

MANAGE PROJECT PROGRESS

Tasks Required to Complete the Step
- Establishing and using a baseline
- Updating tasks
- Updating the schedule
- Setting and updating costs
- Comparing your progress with your plan
- Performing earned value analysis

If you've completed the previous six Steps, you're ready to start tracking the progress of your project. Well, almost. "Step 4: Identify and Allocate Resources" discusses how to estimate resource costs, but doesn't discuss how to estimate task costs, how to record costs, and how to compare actual costs with estimated costs. The latter part of this Step covers these topics.

First, however, we need to look at how you can use a baseline to monitor your progress and how you can record actual information about your schedule and tasks.

Establishing and Using a Baseline

A baseline, as you'll recall from Step 4, is a picture of your final project plan before the start date. You can choose whether or not to save your project with a baseline, but if you do, you can use the baseline as a point of reference when monitoring your project.

Setting the Baseline

You will most likely want to save your project several times before saving the baseline and will want to wait until the final planning stages are complete to save the baseline. To save the baseline, take the following actions:

1. **Choose the Tools menu's Tracking command, and then choose the submenu's Save Baseline command.**

   Project displays the Save Baseline dialog box, as shown in Figure 7-1.

Figure 7-1 The Save Baseline dialog box.

2. **If necessary, click the Save Baseline option button, and then click OK.**

Your other option in the Save Baseline dialog box is to save an interim plan, which you might want to do if your project gets terribly off track. For example, perhaps it starts three months later than you expected. It's important to retain your original baseline because it shows your initial planning, but you also need a way to track your project that is more in line with reality.

> **TIP** A fast way to save the baseline is to click the Track button on the Project Guide toolbar and then click the Save Baseline button in the Save Baseline task pane.

Normally, you'll want to save an interim plan only for tasks that haven't been started. To save an interim plan, take the following actions:

1. Open your project in Gantt Chart view, and select the tasks that have not yet started.

2. Choose the Tools menu's Tracking command, and then choose the submenu's Save Baseline command.

   Project displays the Save Baseline dialog box.

3. Click the Save Interim Plan option button.

4. In the Copy field, click the drop-down arrow, and select a current start-to-finish setting.

5. In the Into field, click the drop-down arrow, and select an interim item.

   WARNING *Don't select the Baseline Start/Finish item in either the Copy field or the Into field. Doing so overwrites your original baseline.*

6. Click the Selected Tasks option button, and then click OK.

To clear a baseline or an interim plan, choose the Tools menu's Tracking command, and then choose the submenu's Clear Baseline command to open the Clear Baseline dialog box, as shown in Figure 7-2. Select what you want to clear, and click OK.

Figure 7-2   The Clear Baseline dialog box.

Changing the Baseline

In general, you don't want to change the baseline, but in certain cases it will be necessary. For example, perhaps you realize after you're into the project that a single task is really two tasks that must be done by two people. To add or modify tasks, use the Entry table in Gantt Chart view, select the tasks, and then save them in the Save Baseline dialog box, following the actions described in the previous section.

Updating Tasks

Before we get into the mechanics of how you update tasks to show what is actually taking place with your project, we need to take a look at the Tracking toolbar, which you can use to quickly enter some common updates. To display the Tracking toolbar, right-click any place in the toolbar area, and select Tracking. Figure 7-3 shows the Tracking toolbar, which contains the following buttons, in left-to-right order:

- Project Statistics
- Update As Scheduled
- Reschedule Work
- Add Progress Line
- 0% Complete
- 25% Complete
- 50% Complete
- 75% Complete
- 100% Complete
- Update Tasks
- Workgroup Toolbar

Figure 7-3 The Tracking toolbar.

NOTE *You'll find information about workgroups in "Step 8: Communicate Project Status."*

Now let's use the Tracking toolbar to enter information about the percentage of tasks complete. Take the following actions:

1. **Open the project in Gantt Chart view.**
2. **Press and hold down the Ctrl key, and select the task or tasks you want to update.**

   Do this by clicking their names in the Task Name column.

3. **Click one of the % Complete buttons on the Tracking toolbar.**

Figure 7-4 shows the book-publishing project with some updated information about the tasks assigned to George. Suppose that George has finished his research and has created the outline. He has started writing Chapter 1 and has about 25% of it done. As you can see, a check mark beside items 2 and 3 indicates that those tasks are 100% complete. The chart shows a dark line through those bars that represent completed or partially completed tasks.

Figure 7-4   The Gantt Chart view shows completed or partially completed tasks.

NOTE   *When you enter a percentage complete for a task, Project updates an actual duration, a remaining duration, and an actual work value.*

Updating the Schedule

As you know, the Gantt Chart view displays your estimated start and finish dates and the durations for tasks. To enter information about how your schedule is actually progressing, you use the Task Details Form view and the Update Tasks dialog box.

Recording Actual Start and Finish Dates

To record the actual dates on which a task starts and finishes, take the following actions:

1. Open your project in Gantt Chart view.
2. Choose the Window menu's Split command.

   Project displays the Task Form view, as shown in Figure 7-5.

Figure 7-5 The book-publishing project open in combination view.

3. **Click in the bottom pane, and then choose the View menu's More Views command.**

   Project displays the More Views dialog box.

4. **Select Task Details Form from the View list, and then click the Apply button.**

   Now your combination view will show the Gantt Chart view in the top pane and the Task Details form in the bottom pane, as shown in Figure 7-6.

Figure 7-6 The Task Details form is displayed in the bottom pane.

5. **Select a task in the top pane.**

   Project displays information about that task in the Task Details form.

6. **Click the Actual option button.**

   Record an actual start or finish date or both.

7. **Click OK.**

   TIP   *To remove the split, choose the Window menu's Remove Split command.*

Step 7   Manage Project Progess   **183**

Recording Actual Durations

You can use the Task Details form to set the actual duration, or you can set the actual duration of a task by clicking the Update Tasks button on the Tracking toolbar and recording information in the Update Tasks dialog box. To use this dialog box, take the following actions:

1. In Gantt Chart view, select the task that you want to update, and click the Update Tasks button on the Tracking toolbar.

   Project displays the Update Tasks dialog box, as shown in Figure 7-7.

Figure 7-7 The Update Tasks dialog box.

2. Fill in information such as the percentage of work completed and the actual and remaining duration, and click OK.

Setting and Updating Costs

Project allows you to assign costs to resources and tasks. You can then total these costs to estimate those project costs that you can directly connect to either a resource or task.

> **NOTE** *Project doesn't really provide a good way of estimating indirect costs—those costs that aren't directly connected to a task or resource. Project also doesn't provide any way to estimate overhead costs—those costs that aren't directly connected to the project and that are only tangentially related. If you want to include these other costs in your cost estimates—and presumably you do—you need to separately account for them.*

Estimating Task Costs

To estimate task costs, you first need to schedule the project, as described in "Step 3: Schedule Project Tasks," and then identify your resources and estimate the resource costs, as described in "Step 4: Identify and Allocate Resources." After you've done this, you can estimate the costs associated with a task by taking the following actions:

1. **Display the Cost table.**

    Display the project in the Gantt Chart view. Then, choose the View menu's Table: Entry command and choose the submenu's Cost command. Project displays the tasks of the project, showing the estimated costs of each, as shown in Figure 7-8.

Figure 7-8 The Cost table.

The estimated resource costs associated with each task will already show. In Figure 7-8, for example, the Write the book task shows a total cost of $11,250. This amount is calculated by totaling the costs of using the resource.

2. **Select the first task for which you want to provide additional cost data.**

    You can select the task by clicking. You can also use the arrow keys.

3. **Provide any fixed cost associated with the task.**

   Click the Fixed Cost box, and then enter any fixed cost associated with this task.

4. **Indicate when the fixed cost is incurred.**

   Use the Fixed Cost Accrual box to indicate when you will incur the fixed cost. The box provides three options: Start, Prorated, and End. Select Start if you incur the fixed cost when the task starts. Select End if you incur the fixed cost when the task ends. Select Prorated if you incur the fixed cost proportionally over the time the task takes.

5. **Describe the other task costs in the project, as necessary.**

   Repeat actions 2 through 4 to describe each of the other task's costs in the project.

As you enter your fixed costs estimates, Project updates the values shown in the Total Cost column.

Reviewing Estimated Project Costs

Once you've estimated the costs of using a resource and any fixed costs associated with tasks, you can view your estimated costs in several useful ways using Project's cost reports.

To view Project's cost reports, take the following actions:

1. **Choose the View menu's Reports command.**

   Project displays the Reports dialog box, as shown in Figure 7-9.

Figure 7-9   The Reports dialog box.

2. **Choose the Costs category.**

   To do this, click Costs and then click the Select button. Project displays the Cost Reports dialog box, as shown in Figure 7-10.

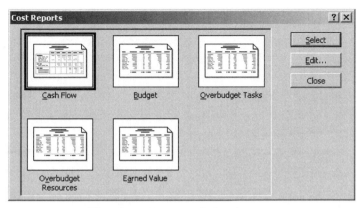

Figure 7-10 The Cost Reports dialog box.

3. Select a cost report.

To see a report, click it and then click the Select button. Project produces an on-screen version of the report. Figure 7-11, for example, shows a Cash Flow report, which shows the cash flows that stem from the costs you estimated for the resources and the costs.

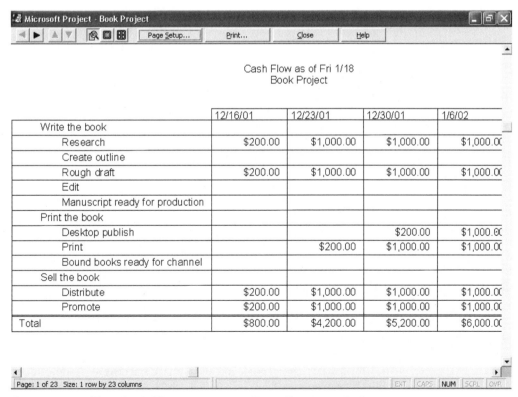

Figure 7-11 The Cash Flow report in a Print Preview window.

NOTE *As you recall from "Step 6: Present Project to Stakeholders," the Project Print Preview window works like the Print Preview window in other Microsoft Windows programs. To print a cost report, choose the Print command. To zoom in and out, click the report. To page through a report, click the Page Right, Page Left, Page Up, and Page Down buttons that appear in the upper left corner of the window and are marked with arrowheads.*

Figure 7-12, for another example, shows a Budget report. It reports on the total estimated costs of each task.

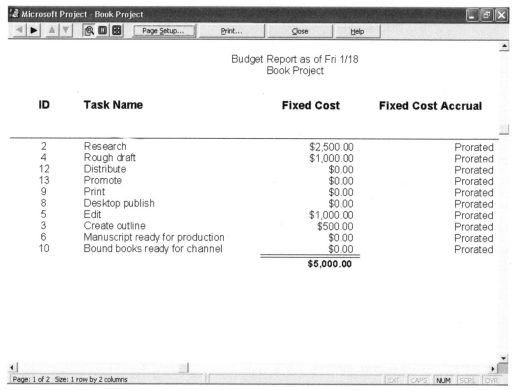

Figure 7-12 The Budget report in a Print Preview window.

Recording Actual Costs

To track actual costs with Project, take the following actions:

1. Display the Cost table.

To do this, first display the project in the Gantt Chart view. Then choose the View menu's Table command, and choose the submenu's Cost command. Project displays the tasks of the project, showing the estimated costs of each, as shown in Figure 7-13.

Figure 7-13 The Cost table.

The Cost table will already be familiar to you if you've used Project to estimate project costs. And, in fact, an advantage of using Project both to estimate costs and track actual costs is that you can then compare budgeted amounts with actual amounts.

NOTE *"Step 4: Identify and Allocate Resources" explains how to estimate resource project costs with Project, and the earlier section "Estimating Task Costs" explains how to estimate task costs.*

2. Select the first task for which you want to record actual cost data.

You can select the task by clicking. You can also use the arrow keys.

3. Record the actual costs associated with the task.

Click the Actual box, and then enter the actual costs associated with this task.

NOTE *You cannot record actual costs for a project unless the task is 100% complete. Note, too, that for tasks that aren't 100% complete, Project estimates the actual costs by multiplying the budgeted costs for the task by the completed percentage for the task. When you mark a task as 100% complete, Project fills in the actual cost with the planned cost. If the actual cost is different from the planned cost, then you'll need to adjust it.*

4. Describe the other actual task costs in the project, as necessary.

Repeat actions 2 and 3 to record the actual costs of each of the other task's costs in the project.

As you record your actual costs, Project updates the values shown in the Total Cost column, as shown in Figure 7-14.

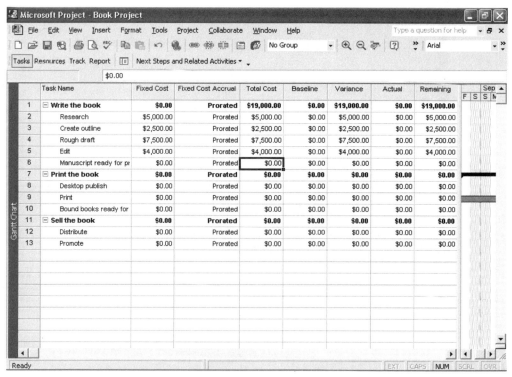

Figure 7-14 The updated Cost table.

Reviewing Actual Project Costs

Once you've recorded actual project costs, you can view your actual costs in several useful ways using Project's Cost reports. For example, you can compare actual costs with budgeted costs.

To view Project's cost reports, take the following actions:

1. **Choose the View menu's Reports command.**

    Project displays the Reports dialog box, as shown in Figure 7-15.

Figure 7-15 The Reports dialog box.

2. **Choose the Costs category.**

    To do this, click Costs and then click the Select button. Project displays the Cost Reports dialog box, as shown in Figure 7-16.

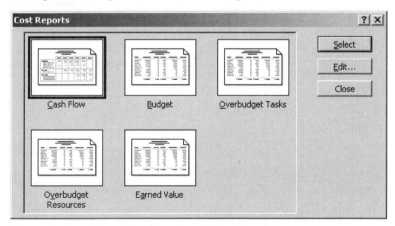

Figure 7-16 The Cost Reports dialog box.

3. Select a cost report.

   To see a report, click it, and then click the Select button. Project produces an on-screen version of the report.

Comparing Your Progress with Your Plan

After you've recorded some actual dates and costs, you can review your progress using still other tools in Project.

Using the Tracking Gantt View

If you want to take a look at the status of the tasks in your project in relationship to the baseline, use the Tracking Gantt view, as shown in Figure 7-17. This view gives you a visual picture of your project's progress. To display your project in Tracking Gantt view, choose the View menu's Gantt Chart comand.

Figure 7-17 A picture of a project's progress in Tracking Gantt view.

Completed tasks or completed portions of tasks appear in dark blue on the chart, and the chart is labeled with percentages.

Using the Work Table

A Work table shows how many person hours are required to complete a task. Work is different from duration, which measures the total time allotted to the task. For example, if the duration of a task is one day, but the total work for the task is 16 hours, you'll need to add resources or extend the duration.

You can use the Work table to show the total time needed from all resources to complete the task. You can display a Work table for tasks and a Work table for resources. In both cases, the table displays baseline information so that you can compare actual to planned progress. To display a Work table for tasks, take the following actions:

1. **Open your project in Gantt Chart view.**
2. **Right-click the Select All button, and choose the shortcut menu's More Tables command.**

    Project displays the More Tables dialog box.

3. **Click the Task option button.**

    If necessary, select Work from the list.

4. **Click the Apply button.**

Figure 7-18 shows the Work table for the tasks in the book-publishing project.

Figure 7-18 A project open in Work table view for tasks.

To display a Work table for resources, take the following actions:

1. **Open your project in Resource Usage view.**

   To do this, choose the View menu's Resource Usage command.

2. **Right-click the Select All button, and choose the shortcut menu's Work command.**

Figure 7-19 shows the book-publishing project open in a Work table for resources.

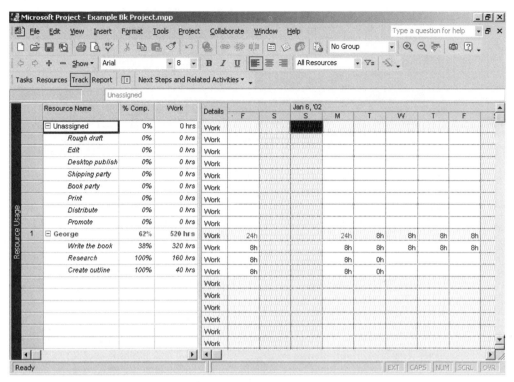

Figure 7-19 A project open in Work table view for resources.

Using Progress Lines

If you have saved a baseline with your project, you can add progress lines to the Gantt chart to connect in-progress tasks. To add a progress line, take the following actions:

1. **Open your project in Gantt Chart view.**
2. **Choose the Tools menu's Tracking command, and then select Progress Lines.**

   Project displays the Progress Lines dialog box, as shown in Figure 7-20.

Figure 7-20 The Progress Lines dialog box.

3. If necessary, click the Dates And Intervals tab.

4. Specify the dates on which to show progress lines.

Select the Display Selected Progress Lines check box, and click Progress Line Dates to display a drop-down calendar.

5. Select a date.

6. Select either Actual Plan or Baseline Plan, and click OK.

Project displays a progress line in the Gantt chart similar to that in Figure 7-21.

Figure 7-21 A progress line displayed in a Gantt chart.

Performing Earned Value Analysis

If you use Project to estimate and record costs and to track progress and you save project baseline information, you can also perform *earned value analysis*. In a nutshell, earned value analysis compares the percentages of work completed with the percentages of costs incurred. Table 7-1 summarizes the information that earned value analysis provides.

VALUE	DESCRIPTION
BCWS	An acronym for the Budgeted Cost of Work Scheduled. This amount shows the planned value of the work originally scheduled.
BCWP	An acronym for Budgeted Cost of Work Performed. This amount shows the planned value of the work completed.
ACWP	An acronym for Actual Cost of Work Performed. This amount shows the actual value, or cost, of the work completed.
SV	An acronym for Schedule Variance. This amount shows the difference between the BCWS and the BCWP.
CV	An acronym for Cost Variance. This amount shows the difference between BCWP and ACWP.
EAC	An acronym for Estimated At Completion. This amount shows the total actual cost incurred to date plus the remaining planned costs.
BAC	An acronym for Budgeted At Completion. This amount shows the total planned cost.
VAC	An acronym for Variance At Completion. This amount shows the difference between the BAC and the EAC.

Table 7-1   Amounts reported by earned value analysis.

NOTE *"Step 1: Learn the Language" describes what earned value analysis is and how it works.*

Viewing the Earned Value Tables

You can view earned value analysis information for resources and for tasks. To view an Earned Value table for resources, take the following actions:

1. Display the Resource Sheet.

You can do this by clicking the Resource Sheet icon on the View bar.

2. Tell Project you want to view the earned value table for resources.

You can do this by right-clicking the Select All button and choosing the shortcut menu's More Tables command. Then when Project displays the More Tables dialog box, click Earned Value and then click the Apply button. Project then displays the Earned Value table for resources.

To view an Earned Value table for tasks, take the following actions:

1. **Display the Task Sheet.**

   You can do this by displaying the Gantt Chart view or one of the other task views. To display the Gantt Chart view, click the Gantt Chart icon on the View bar.

2. **Tell Project you want to view the Earned Value table for tasks.**

   You can do this by right-clicking the Select All button and choosing the shortcut menu's More Tables command. Then when Project displays the More Tables dialog box, click Earned Value and click the Apply button. Project then displays the Earned Value table for tasks, as shown in Figure 7-22.

	Task Name	BCWS	BCWP	ACWP	SV	CV	EAC	BAC	VAC
1	**Write the book**	**$0.00**	**$0.00**	**$8,400.00**	**$0.00**	**($8,400.00)**	**$14,150.00**	**$0.00**	**($14,150.00)**
2	Research	$0.00	$0.00	$7,800.00	$0.00	($7,800.00)	$7,800.00	$0.00	($7,800.00)
3	Create outline	$0.00	$0.00	$600.00	$0.00	($600.00)	$600.00	$0.00	($600.00)
4	Rough draft	$0.00	$0.00	$0.00	$0.00	$0.00	$4,000.00	$0.00	($4,000.00)
5	Edit	$0.00	$0.00	$0.00	$0.00	$0.00	$1,750.00	$0.00	($1,750.00)
6	**Print the book**	**$0.00**	**$0.00**	**$0.00**	**$0.00**	**$0.00**	**$10,100.00**	**$0.00**	**($10,100.00)**
7	Desktop publish	$0.00	$0.00	$0.00	$0.00	$0.00	$700.00	$0.00	($700.00)
8	Shipping party	$0.00	$0.00	$0.00	$0.00	$0.00	$400.00	$0.00	($400.00)
9	Book party	$0.00	$0.00	$0.00	$0.00	$0.00	$400.00	$0.00	($400.00)
10	Print	$0.00	$0.00	$0.00	$0.00	$0.00	$8,600.00	$0.00	($8,600.00)
11	**Sell the book**	**$0.00**	**$0.00**	**$0.00**	**$0.00**	**$0.00**	**$4,910.00**	**$0.00**	**($4,910.00)**
12	Distribute	$0.00	$0.00	$0.00	$0.00	$0.00	$4,500.00	$0.00	($4,500.00)
13	Promote	$0.00	$0.00	$0.00	$0.00	$0.00	$410.00	$0.00	($410.00)

Figure 7-22 The Earned Value table for tasks.

Viewing an Earned Value Report

One of the other tools that Project provides for reviewing earned value analysis information is to the Earned Value report. To view the Earned Value report, take the following actions:

1. **Choose the View menu's Reports command.**

   Project displays the Reports dialog box.

2. **Choose the Costs category.**

   To do this, click Costs and then click the Select button. Project displays the Cost Reports dialog box.

3. **Select the Earned Value report.**

   Click Earned Value, and then click the Select button. Project produces an on-screen version of the report.

Summary

This Step looked at the many ways you can monitor the progress of your project in Project. One thing it didn't mention, however, is how you acquire the information you record in the various tables and dialog boxes. If your organization is sizable and you are not on a local area network, an intranet, or the Internet, getting the information you need may require some legwork or a procedure that ensures that you get regular status reports from those working on the project. "Step 8: Communicate Project Status" looks at how you can use workgroups and a network. Working over a network can simplify the job of collecting update information, although you'll still have to enter it in Project.

Step 8

COMMUNICATE PROJECT STATUS

Tasks Required to Complete the Step
- Exchanging Project information by e-mail
- Sending a project file to someone else
- Routing a project file

As you complete a project, you need to keep the team members apprised of the task status. Although traditional means of communication (face-to-face meetings, telephone calls, letters) may work well for some tasks, other times you might want to immediately communicate detailed information about a project to people in diverse areas. To facilitate doing so, Microsoft Project has built-in e-mail features allowing you to quickly and easily send e-mail regarding project status. Project also allows you to send special e-mail task requests, task updates, and status reports.

A Word about Microsoft Project Server and Project Central

This Step addresses how to communicate about the status of a project by e-mail, but Project offers a couple other ways to engage in team efforts—with Microsoft Project Server and the Project Central Service. These features involve setting up Internet or intranet Web sites and collaborating with others online. Both features are beyond the scope of this little book, but we will describe them briefly so you know what's what. If your organization has chosen to work by way of Microsoft Project Server or Project Central, ask your system administrator for details about working this way.

Microsoft Project Server is a companion product to Project. After the Web server has been set up, collaborators can open their browsers to a Web site, see if tasks have been assigned to them, and learn the status of the project they are working on. Most of the commands that are available in Project can be undertaken at the Web site. A so-called Project manager administers the Web site.

Project Central is similar to Project Server in that collaboration also takes place on the Internet or an intranet. The difference, however, is that not as many tasks can be accomplished and setting up a Web server isn't necessary.

Declaring How You Want to Collaborate

Whether you collaborate with others by e-mail or Microsoft Project Server, your first step is to tell Project how you want to collaborate. You do that by using the Collaborate tab of the Options dialog box:

1. **Choose the Tools menu's Options command.**

    The Options dialog box appears.

2. **Click the Collaborate tab.**

    Figure 8-1 shows this tab.

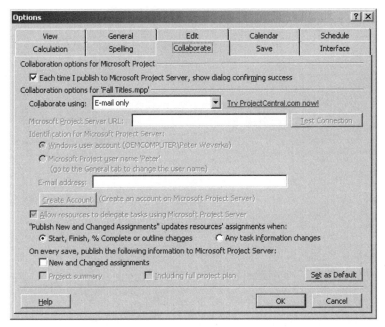

Figure 8-1 The Collaborate tab of the Options dialog box.

3. **On the Collaborate Using drop-down menu, choose an option and click OK.**

   For example, choose E-Mail Only if your organization does not collaborate by way of Microsoft Project Server or the Project Central Service.

Getting Ready to Collaborate by E-Mail

To communicate about a project file via a network e-mail system, you first need to make sure that all of the workgroup members (the resources involved in the project) have a MAPI-compliant, 32-bit e-mail client, such as Outlook or Outlook Express.

Then you need to make sure that any team members who don't have Project installed on their computers run the file WGSETUP.EXE, which is located on the Project CD-ROM. This file sets up a program by which team members can collaborate. Instead of conventional e-mail forms, team members see forms like the one in Figure 8-2. They do not have to enter e-mail addresses. All they have to do is write replies and click the Send button.

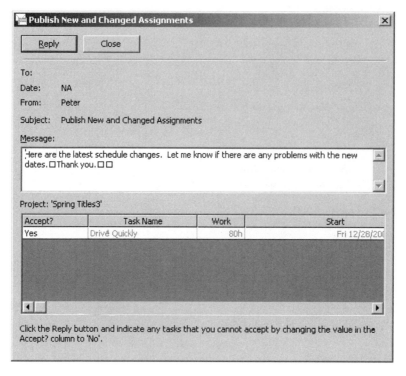

Figure 8-2 Communicating by e-mail about a project.

Recording Your Collaborators' E-Mail Addresses

It goes without saying, but you can't trade e-mail with collaborators until you have entered their e-mail addresses in your Address Book or at least told Project what their e-mail addresses are. If a collaborator's address is on file in your Address Book already, you don't have to enter it. Take these actions to make sure that you have all of the workgroup members' e-mail addresses stored in your Address Book:

1. **Open the Project file containing the resources with whom you want to communicate via e-mail.**

   If you're using a resource pool across multiple projects, open the resource pool.

   NOTE *"Step 4: Identify and Allocate Resources" describes setting up and working with resource pools.*

2. **Display the Resource Sheet.**

   Choose the View menu's Resource Sheet command to display the Resource Sheet if you're not currently displaying it.

3. **Double-click the resource with whom you want to communicate via e-mail.**

   Project displays the General tab of the Resource Information dialog box, as shown in Figure 8-3.

Figure 8-3 Setting up a resource to receive e-mail about a project.

4. **Select E-Mail Only from the Workgroup drop-down list box.**

5. **Click the Details button.**

   If Project finds a contact in your Address Book that matches the resource's name, it displays the properties for that contact. If Project can't find a resource, it displays the Check Names dialog box, as shown in Figure 8-4.

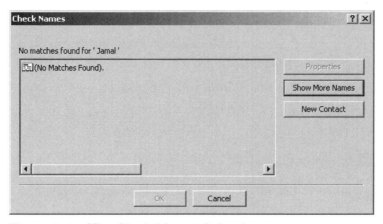

Figure 8-4 The Check Names dialog box.

NOTE *If Project finds multiple entries that match the name you entered, it lists them in the Check Names dialog box. Select the correct entry, and click OK.*

- Click the Show More Names button if you believe that you have the resource's e-mail address in your Address Book. Project allows you to view the list of contacts in your Address Book and select the correct one.
- Click the Create A New Address option button to create a new contact entry.

Assigning Tasks or Projects by E-Mail

After you assign a task or project to a workgroup member via e-mail and request a response, the task request recipient can either accept or decline the request. If he or she doesn't reply, Project assumes that he or she has accepted the assignment. To assign a project or task by e-mail, take the following actions:

1. **Display in Gantt Chart view the project containing the tasks you want to assign.**
2. **If you want to assign only some tasks, select those tasks.**
3. **Choose the Collaborate menu's Publish command, and then choose New and Changed Assignments from the submenu.**

   You see the Publish New And Changed Assignments dialog box shown in Figure 8-5. It lists the names of resources (people in this case) who will be sent task assignments, when they are due, and so on.

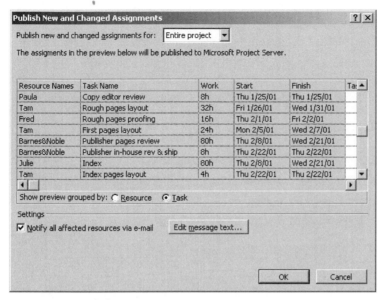

Figure 8-5 The Publish New And Changed Assignments dialog box.

TIP *To assign one task only, right-click it and choose Publish New And Change Information on the shortcut menu. You will see the Publish New And Changed Assignments dialog box.*

4. Click the Edit Message Text button and enter a word or two about the assignment.

You see the Edit Message Text dialog box shown in Figure 8-6. From here, you can describe the assignment in a little more detail or enter a word of encouragement.

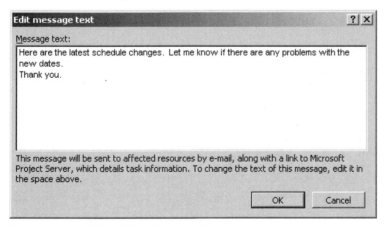

Figure 8-6 The Edit Message Text dialog box.

5. **Click OK to send the message.**

   Project places the task assignment message in your Outbox. Depending on the services you use and how you have your e-mail client set up, you may need to deliver the message by clicking a button in your e-mail program or by making a dial-up connection to the Internet. The message is sent as a file attachment.

   NOTE *Project sends the file as an .MTM attachment.*

Figure 8-7 shows what a task assignment looks like to the person who receives it. As explained earlier, the recipient must have run the WGSETUP.EXE setup program on his or her computer to see the dialog box shown in Figure 8-7. When the recipient opens the file attachment you sent, he or she sees this dialog box.

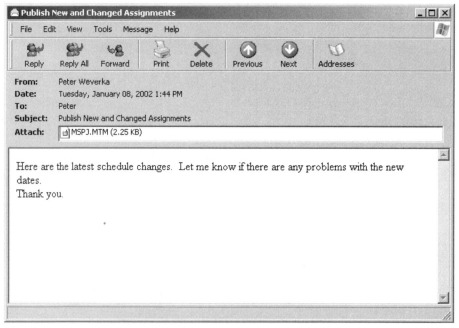

Figure 8-7 A task assignment e-mail message.

To reply to a task assignment message, open the message, click the Reply button, and leave the default of Yes in the Accept? box to accept the request or enter No in the Accept? box to decline the request. To enter No, the recipient can double-click the Accept? box. Then click the Send button. When you receive a reply to a task request, open the message and click Update Project to update the project.

Updating Task Assignments

What happens when someone responds to a task you assigned by e-mail? The response lands in your e-mail program's Inbox as an attached file. When you open the attached file, you see the Re: Publish New And Changed Assignments dialog box, as shown in Figure 8-8. This dialog box tells you to whom you assigned the task, the project file you are working with, and the name of the task. From here, you can either respond to the request with an e-mail message or update your Project file:

- Click the Reply button to send an e-mail message. After you click this button, the Re: Publish New And Changed Assignments dialog box gives you space to enter a message. Enter it and click the Send button.

- Click the Update Project button to let Project know that you have received a response. The mail icon that appears in Gantt Chart view when you send a task assignment disappears to let you know that the assignment has been taken care of.

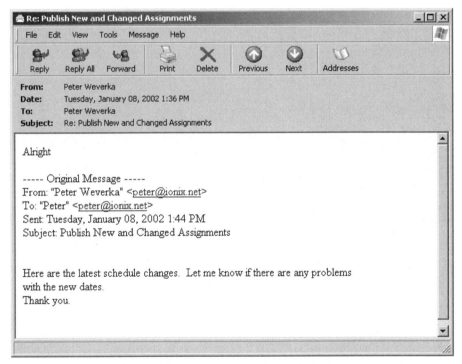

Figure 8-8   The Re: Publish New And Changed Assignments dialog box.

Step 8 Communicate Project Status

Requesting Progress Information about a Task

Besides assigning a task to workgroup members, you can send them e-mails asking to know how a project is coming along. Project offers a special command for doing just that—the Request Project Information command. This command works exactly like the Publish New And Changed Assignments command. However, instead of assigning a task, you merely ask your collaborator how the task is going.

To give the command, right-click a task in Gantt Chart view and choose Request Progress Information on the shortcut menu. Then, in the Request Progress Information dialog box, click the Edit Message Text button, enter a word or two, and click OK.

Sending a Project File

To send a Project file as an e-mail message attachment, open the File menu's Send To command, and then choose Mail Recipient (As Attachment) on the submenu. You see a new message form in your default e-mail program, whatever it happens to be. Address and complete the message in the usual way. Figure 8-9 shows a message filled out in Microsoft Outlook Express. In Outlook Express, you click the Send toolbar button to send the message.

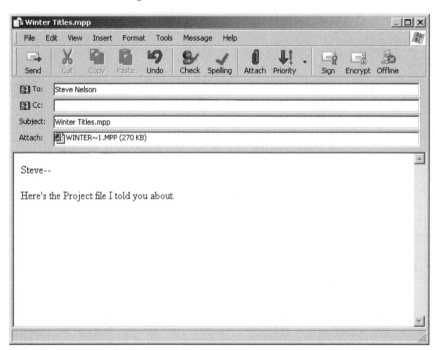

Figure 8-9 Sending a Project file as an e-mail attachment.

> **NOTE** *If you send a Project 2002 file as an attachment, the message recipient must have Project 2002 to be able to read the file. If the recipient doesn't have this version, you need to save the file in a different format and then attach the file to a new message from your e-mail client.*

Routing a File to Others

Besides sending a Project file, you can route it to a group of people. Route a file by e-mail when you want others to have a look at it. Routing means telling Project the name of each reviewer and the order in which you want reviewers to get the file. When the file arrives in reviewers' mailboxes, it does so along with this message: "The project below has a routing slip. When you are done reviewing this project, choose Next Routing Recipient from the Send To menu in the Microsoft Project File menu to continue the routing."

After a reviewer has looked over the file, he or she sends it to the next person on the routing list. Others can send the Project file merely by choosing the File menu's Send To command and choosing Next Routing Recipient on the submenu. Meanwhile, a message arrives in your e-mail box each time the file is sent to the next person on the routing list. The message tells you that the file has been sent and in whose hands the Project file is now.

To route a file to several reviewers, choose the File menu's Send To command, and then choose Routing Recipient on the submenu. You see the Routing Slip dialog box shown in Figure 8-10.

Figure 8-10 The Routing Slip dialog box.

Click the Address button to select recipients from your Address Book. After you have selected the recipients, use the Routing Slip dialog box's Move buttons to move recipients up and down in the route. Click the Route button to route the messages. Click the Add Slip button to add the routing slip to the project and close the Routing Slip dialog box.

If you work on a network with a Microsoft Exchange server, you can post a Project file to a public folder by clicking the Send To Exchange Folder toolbar button.

NOTE *To post to an Exchange folder, you need to have an e-mail client capable of working with the Microsoft Exchange Server service (such as Outlook) installed as your default e-mail client.*

Summary

In this Step we looked at the ways you can use e-mail to communicate project status with workgroup members. This is the final activity of creating a project. In the appendixes of this book, we describe how to use Project's tools for working with complex projects, how to link multiple projects, and how to customize Project to suit your needs.

Appendix A

DEAL WITH PROJECT COMPLEXITY

In This Appendix
- Simplifying dependency relationships
- Dividing a large project into multiple subprojects
- Using WBS codes
- Using macros to automate actions

The simple approach described in the steps of this book works for most projects. In our own experiences, such a "keep it simple" approach works well even when projects become more complex because the number of tasks, dependences, constraints, and resources grow.

In a certain number of cases, unfortunately, you will need to complicate your project plans to deal with the realities of a project. This appendix describes some of the tools that Microsoft Project 2002 supplies for recognizing and dealing with these real-world complexities.

Simplifying Dependency Relationships

You can often avoid the sort of fine-tuning of task durations described in "Step 3: Schedule Project Tasks" by working with complete and detailed sets of tasks. This is especially true if you begin to use lag time in your relationships. Lag time often indicates that you're either working with incomplete detail in your tasks or missing tasks.

In some cases, when you work with dependency relationships other than the standard finish-to-start relationship and include lag time, it's because one of the tasks in the relationship is really a summary task. And what you're doing is trying to show that one part of the predecessor task needs to finish before the successor task or one part of the successor task can start.

Take the case of a book manuscript, for example. You might say at first blush that the book manuscript needs to be written before it can be edited. And then, when confronted with the need to compress the schedule in order to meet some deadline, you might say that, well, you can actually start editing while the writer is still writing.

Given the scenario described in the preceding paragraph, you might decide that rather than working with a standard finish-to-start dependency relationship, you can work with a start-to-start dependency relationship as long as the start of the successor task lags the start of the predecessor by, say, one week.

Often, however, a better way to deal with this reality—the reality that the editor can start working before the writer is finished writing—is to break the writing and editing tasks into smaller subtasks. A Write Manuscript task might be broken into two subtasks: Write Chapters 1 to 5 and Write Chapters 6 to 10. An Edit Manuscript task might similarly be broken into two subtasks: Edit Chapters 1 to 5 and Edit Chapters 6 to 10.

Once the project schedule more closely matches reality, it's easy to work with simple finish-to-start dependency relationships and zero lag times. The Write Chapters 1 to 5 task needs to finish before the Edit Chapters 1 to 5 task can start. The Write Chapters 6 to 10 task needs to finish before the Edit Chapters 6 to 10 task can start. In both dependencies, the relationship is finish-to-start and the lag time equals zero.

Lag times may also indicate that a project schedule is simply missing a task. For example, suppose you're working with a two-task project for painting some interior office space. The first and predecessor task might be Paint Office. The second and successor task might be Clean Up. In this scenario, you might use a lag time equal to the time required for the paint to dry.

Another option—often preferable because it's simpler—is to create a task for Let Paint Dry. In this case, you then work with three tasks, all with finish-to-start dependency relationships, and all with zero-lag-time settings. What's more, replacing the lag time with an actual task, Let Paint Dry, explains and highlights the lag time.

We recommend you adopt the strategy of working with detailed task lists as a way to minimize the sort of complexity that comes from dependency fine-tuning. If you do adopt such a strategy, however, you end up with voluminous numbers of project tasks. To deal with this drawback, you probably want to use summary tasks in your schedules. Using summary tasks will make it easy to present project schedule information in a summarized fashion—something that will probably make project management and project reporting easier.

> **NOTE** *"Step 3: Schedule Project Tasks" explains how to create and use summary tasks.*

Dividing a Large Project into Multiple Subprojects

If you have a complex project with many tasks, you can create subprojects and save them as separate files to work with them independently and focus on one area at a time. To create subprojects from a large project, take the following actions:

1. **Display the large project file in Gantt Chart view.**

   To do this, choose the View menu's Gantt Chart command.

2. **Select the tasks you want to save in the first subproject file, and click the Copy toolbar button.**

   Project copies the tasks you selected to the Clipboard.

3. **Click the New toolbar button to create a new file.**

4. **Click the Paste toolbar button.**

5. **Save the subproject.**

6. **Redisplay the large project file, and repeat the procedure for subsequent subproject files.**

> **NOTE** *"Appendix B: Work with Multiple Projects" describes how you can link tasks across separate project files. "Step 4: Identify and Allocate Resources" describes how you can share a resource pool among multiple project files.*

Using WBS Codes

It often helps to outline complex projects using a system called Work Breakdown Structure, or WBS. WBS codes number tasks according to their position in the outline. For example, if your project is writing and printing a book, the tasks might be as follows:

1. Research the topic.
2. Create the outline.
3. Write the rough draft.
4. Edit the rough draft.
5. Desktop-publish the manuscript.
6. Ship the book to the printer
7. Distribute the book to booksellers.
8. Promote the book.

The WBS code for the first task is just 1. If this first task includes the following subtasks:

1. Establish research goals.
2. Obtain research materials.
3. Read research materials.
4. Gather notes about materials.

then these tasks would have the WBS codes 1.1, 1.2, 1.3, and 1.4, respectively.

To display WBS codes in Project, take the following actions:

1. **Choose the Tools menu's Options command, and click the View tab.**

   Project displays the Options dialog box, as shown in Figure A-1.

   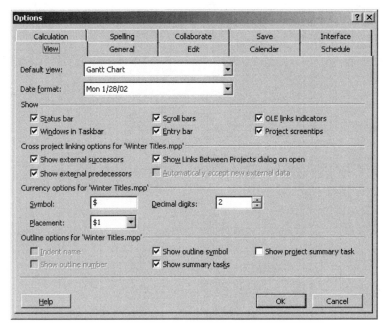

   Figure A-1 The View tab of the Options dialog box.

2. **Select the Show Outline Number check box, and click OK.**

   Figure A-2 shows how the example book project looks with WBS codes displayed. Notice the outline numbers.

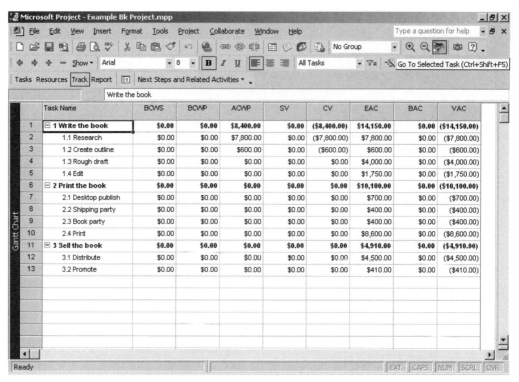

Figure A-2 A project with WBS codes.

To insert a column for the WBS codes, choose the Insert menu's Column command. In the Column Definition dialog box, select WBS from the Field Name drop-down list box and click OK.

If your company uses customized WBS codes for project management, you can define these codes in Project. To do so, choose the Project menu's WBS command and choose the submenu's Define Code command. Project displays the WBS Code Definition dialog box for the current project, as shown in Figure A-3. Use this dialog box to specify the code mask for each level. The Code Preview box shows what your choices mean in real terms.

Figure A-3 The WBS Code Definition dialog box.

NOTE *WBS codes work much like the outline codes described in "Step 7: Manage Project Progress," except outline codes do not necessarily match the outline structure of your project, as do WBS codes. For example, you can create outline codes based on your company's cost codes. For more information about outline codes and specifying code masks, see Step 7.*

Using Macros to Automate Actions

You can speed your work in complex projects by using macros to automate repetitive tasks. If you have programming experience, you can write your macro in Microsoft Visual Basic for Applications. You can also create a program by recording a series of actions into a macro.

NOTE *To program in Visual Basic for Applications, choose the Tools menu's Macro command and choose the submenu's Visual Basic Editor command.*

To record a macro, take the following actions:

1. **Plan and practice the actions you want to record.**

   Go through the actions, and, if necessary, take notes to remember the order of actions you want to record.

2. **Choose the Tools menu's Macro command, and choose the submenu's Record New Macro command.**

   Project displays the Record Macro dialog box, as shown in Figure A-4.

Figure A-4 The Record Macro dialog box.

3. **Name the macro.**

   The macro name must begin with a letter and not a number or other character. Macro names cannot contain spaces.

4. **Optionally, assign a keyboard shortcut to the macro.**

   Enter a letter in the Shortcut Key box. If you select a letter that Project already uses to perform an action, Project displays a warning and requires that you choose a different letter. For example, the Ctrl+S combination is the keyboard shortcut for saving. If you enter *S* in the dialog box, Project displays a warning when you click OK.

5. **Specify the storage location for the macro.**

    To make a macro available to all projects, select Global File from the Store Macro In drop-down list box. To make the macro available in only the current project, select This Project from the Store Macro In drop-down list box.

    NOTE *If you store a macro in the current project and later want to copy the macro to a template for use in other projects, you can use Project's Organizer feature. Choose the Tools menu's Organizer command, and click the Modules tab.*

6. **Describe the macro.**

7. **Specify how the macro should select rows and columns.**
    - Click the Relative option button in the Row References section if you want the macro to begin with the selected cell when it is run.
    - Click the Absolute (ID) option button if you want the macro to always begin in the same row, regardless of which cell is selected when the macro is run.
    - Click the Absolute (Field) option button in the Column References section if you want the macro to always begin in the same row, regardless of which cell is selected when the macro is run.
    - Click the Relative option button if you want the macro to begin with the selected cell.

8. **Click OK.**

    Project begins recording your actions.

    TIP *Project does not record the pace of your actions, so time is not of the essence. Take your time to complete the actions carefully rather than hurrying and needing to record the macro again.*

9. **When you're finished, choose the Tools menu's Macro command and choose the submenu's Stop Recorder command.**

    Project stops recording your macro and saves the macro in the location you specified.

To run the macro, choose the Tools menu's Macro command and choose the submenu's Macros command to open the dialog box shown in Figure A-5.

Figure A-5 The Macros dialog box.

Select the macro you want to run from the Macro Name list, and click the Run button. Project performs the actions you recorded.

> **TIP** *If you assigned a keyboard shortcut to the macro, you can quickly run the macro by pressing the shortcut key. You can also create a custom toolbar button for a macro. For more information about creating custom toolbar buttons, see "Appendix C: Customize Project."*

Appendix B

WORK WITH MULTIPLE PROJECTS

In This Appendix
- Creating a consolidated project file for multiple projects
- Updating links of source projects
- Linking tasks across separate project files

If you manage more than one project at a time, chances are high that the projects interact in some way. Perhaps a task in one project depends on a task in another. Or perhaps resources require leveling across all projects. Luckily, Microsoft Project 2002 allows you to consolidate multiple projects into one large file so you can work with numerous projects together.

NOTE *The same feature that allows you to consolidate multiple projects also lets you divide a large project into more manageable subprojects and work with the subprojects individually.*

Creating a Consolidated Project File for Multiple Projects

To consolidate Project files into one large Project file with multiple subprojects, take the following actions:

1. **Create a new project file for the consolidated project.**

   NOTE *Although you can use an existing Project file as the consolidated Project file, it doesn't usually make sense to do so because you will no longer be able to work with the existing project independent from the other subprojects included in the consolidated file.*

2. **Display the file in Gantt Chart view.**

   To do so, choose the View menu's Gantt Chart command.

3. **Select the Task Name box for the row where you want to insert the subproject.**

   If your consolidated Project file contains tasks, select the task above which you want the subproject inserted.

4. **Choose the Insert menu's Project command.**

   Project displays the Insert Project dialog box, as shown in Figure B-1.

Figure B-1   The Insert Project dialog box.

5. **Open the folder storing the file.**

   Use the icons along the left side of the Insert Project dialog box and the list box of folders and files to locate the file. When you find it, select it by clicking it.

6. **Specify whether you want to link or embed the subproject.**

   Select the Link To Project check box if you want changes in the consolidated project file updated in the subproject file and vice versa. Clear the Link To Project check box if you want to simply paste the subproject into the consolidated Project file.

7. **Click the Insert button.**

   Project inserts the subproject in the row above the selected row, as shown in Figure B-2. The Information column displays an icon reminding you that the subproject is inserted from another file. If you rest your mouse pointer over the icon, Project displays a ScreenTip that describes the link.

   Figure B-2 Creating a consolidated Project file.

8. **Repeat actions 3 through 7 for other projects you want to insert in the consolidated project.**

9. **If you want to work with the consolidated project again, save it after you're finished inserting projects.**

   You can work with the tasks in a consolidated Project file the same way you work with tasks in all other Project files. For example, you link tasks (regardless of the subproject to which they belong) as described in "Step 3: Schedule Project Tasks." If you make changes to the consolidated project and if you chose to link to the source projects when you initially created the consolidated project, Project asks you whether you want to save changes to each of the source projects.

   TIP *To focus on certain subprojects, you can hide others. Just click the minus sign beside the subproject's summary task.*

Updating Links of Source Projects

If you chose to link the source projects to the consolidated project, you will need to update the links if you move the source file. To do so, take the following actions:

1. **Open the consolidated Project file.**

   If necessary, choose the View menu's Gantt Chart command to display the file in Gantt Chart view.

2. **Select the project you need to relink.**

   To do so, click the inserted project's name in the Task Name column.

3. **Click the Task Information toolbar button.**

   Project displays the Inserted Project Information dialog box.

4. **Click the Advanced tab.**

   Figure B-3 shows the Advanced tab of the Inserted Project Information dialog box.

Figure B-3   The Inserted Project Information dialog box.

5. **Specify the new path to the source file.**

   Enter a new location in the Link To Project text box, or click the Browse button to locate the source file.

   TIP   *To unlink the source file, clear the Link To Project check box.*

6. **Click OK.**

Linking Tasks Across Separate Project Files

If you don't want to create a consolidated project, you can still link tasks across projects. To do so, you need to create external links. To work with external links, take the following actions:

1. **Open the project containing the task you want to link to another file.**

   If necessary, display the project in Gantt Chart view.

2. **Click in the Predecessors column for the task you want to link.**

3. **Enter the path to the project, a backslash, and the task ID number within that project.**

   For example, if the task to which you want to link is number 6 in a project named September in your My Documents folder, you would enter the following:

   C:\MY DOCUMENTS\SEPTEMBER.MPP\6

   Figure B-4 shows an example of an external link in a project.

Figure B-4 Linking a task to a task in an external project.

NOTE *You edit external links the same way you edit internal links. "Step 3: Schedule Project Tasks" describes editing links.*

Appendix C

CUSTOMIZE PROJECT

In This Appendix
- Customizing toolbars
- Customizing menus
- Customizing a table
- Customizing the Gantt chart
- Changing the default view

As you work with Microsoft Project 2002 and become more familiar with it, you'll probably eventually wish that you could change certain features. You might, for example, prefer that your project always opens in a view other than the Gantt Chart view, or you might want to replace the Task Notes button with another button that you'd actually use. The good new is that you can change most of the elements in Project, and in this appendix we walk you through the steps.

Customizing Toolbars

By default, Project displays the Standard and Formatting toolbars. To hide either of these or display other toolbars, you choose the View menu's Toolbars command and then click the name of a toolbar on the submenu to hide or display it. In addition, you can add and remove buttons from the default toolbar, and you can even create completely new toolbars.

Adding and Deleting Buttons

You can add and delete toolbar buttons from the default toolbars in a couple of ways. Let's look at the simplest and quickest way first. At the far right on each of the default toolbars, you'll see a little down arrow. When you place your cursor over this arrow, you'll see a ScreenTip that tells you this is the More Buttons button. When you click the More Buttons button, you'll see the Add Or Remove Buttons button. Clicking this button displays a drop-down list of the available buttons for that toolbar. Figure C-1 shows the available buttons for the Standard toolbar. A check mark preceding a button name indicates that the button is currently displayed. To remove the button, simply click its name. To restore a button, click its name again.

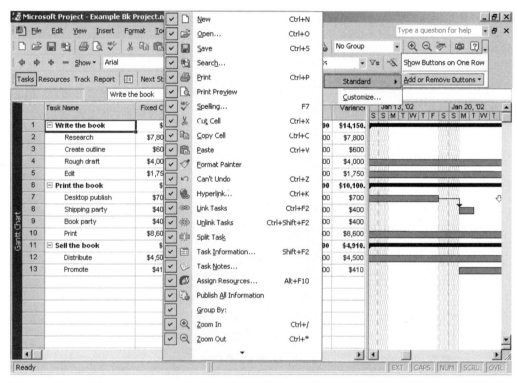

Figure C-1 The buttons on the Standard toolbar.

But what if you want to, for example, display a Tracking toolbar button on the Standard toolbar? To add a button to a toolbar, take the following actions:

1. **Choose the Tools menu's Customize command, and then choose the submenu's Toolbars command.**

   Project displays the Customize dialog box, as shown in Figure C-2.

230   *Project 2002: Effective Project Management in Eight Steps*

Figure C-2 The Customize dialog box.

2. **If necessary, click the Toolbars tab.**

3. **Make sure that the toolbar that contains the button you want to add is displayed.**

   If it is not selected, click the toolbar's check box.

4. **Click the Commands tab.**

   Project displays the Commands tab of the Customize dialog box, as shown in Figure C-3.

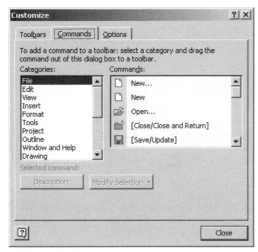

Figure C-3 The Commands tab of the Customize dialog box.

5. **Select the category that contains the command you want to add.**

   In the Categories list, select the toolbar button you want to add.

6. **Click the command, and then drag it to the toolbar on which you want to display it.**

   Project adds the button to the toolbar.

7. **Click Close in the Customize dialog box.**

   To delete a button from a toolbar, open the Customize dialog box and then click and drag the button off the toolbar.

   TIP *To restore a toolbar to its original settings, open the Customize dialog box, select the name of the toolbar, and click the Reset button.*

Changing Button Images

If you were designing the Project interface, would you have chosen some different little pictures for some of the buttons? Well, to a certain extent, you can play designer. You can change a button's image to one of the other predefined images that are included with Project, and you can edit those images.

Selecting a New Image

To select a new image for an existing toolbar button, take the following actions:

1. **Display the toolbar that contains the button whose image you want to change.**

   To display a toolbar, choose the View menu's Toolbars command and then choose the toolbar from the submenu.

2. **Choose the Tools menu's Customize command, and then choose the submenu's Toolbars command.**

   Project displays the Customize dialog box.

3. **Click the Commands tab.**

4. **Click the button for which you want to select a new image.**

   In other words, move the pointer out of the dialog box and click the toolbar button that needs changing.

5. **Click the Modify Selection button, and then choose Change Button Image.**

   Project displays a palette of button images, as shown in Figure C-4.

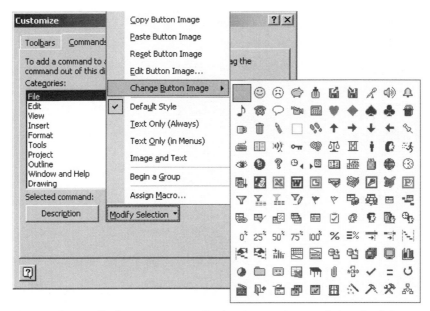

Figure C-4 Click an image to display it on a button instead of the current image.

6. Click Close in the Customize dialog box.

To restore a button's original image, take actions 1 through 3, click the Modify Selection button, choose Reset Button Image, and then click Close in the Customize dialog box.

Editing an Image

If you want to edit a current image instead of selecting a new image, take the following actions:

1. **Display the toolbar that contains the button whose image you want to edit.**

   To display a toolbar, choose the View menu's Toolbars command and then choose the toolbar from the submenu.

2. **Choose the Tools menu's Customize command, and then choose the submenu's Toolbars command.**

   Project displays the Customize dialog box.

3. **Click the Commands tab.**

4. **Click the button for which you want to select a new image.**

   That's right—move the pointer outside the dialog box and click a button.

5. Click the Modify Selection button, and then choose Edit Button Image.

Project displays the Button Editor dialog box, as shown in Figure C-5.

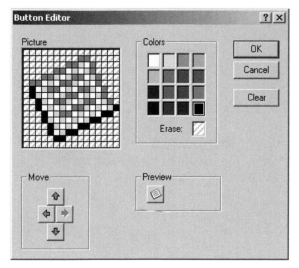

Figure C-5   The Button Editor dialog box.

6. To change the colors of an image, click a color and then click a pixel in the picture.

NOTE   *An image is composed of many tiny squares, as you can see in Figure C-5. Each square is called a* pixel *(short for* picture element*).*

7. To remove color from a pixel, click the Erase square and then click the pixel.
8. If you can't see all of a large button in the Picture box, click an arrow in the Move box.
9. When you've finished redesigning the button, click OK.

Click Close when you're finished to close the Customize dialog box.

Creating a New Toolbar

If you're working on a project that involves using a number of buttons often and these buttons are on various toolbars, you might want to consider creating a new toolbar that includes only these buttons. To do so, take the following actions:

1. Choose the Tools menu's Customize command, and then choose the submenu's Toolbars command.

Project displays the Customize dialog box.

2. Click New.

   Project displays the New Toolbar dialog box, as shown in Figure C-6.

   Figure C-6   The New Toolbar dialog box.

3. **Enter a name for your toolbar in the Toolbar Name box (perhaps the name of your project), and click OK.**

   A small toolbar will appear on your screen, as shown in Figure C-7. You can move this toolbar to any location on the screen that you like. Simply click the title bar and then drag the toolbar. In addition, you'll see that the name of your new toolbar has been added to the Toolbars list in the Toolbars tab.

Figure C-7   You can drag tools to populate the toolbar you just created.

Appendix C   Customize Project   **235**

NOTE *You may need to move the Customize dialog box in order to see your new toolbar.*

4. **Click the Commands tab.**
5. **Select a category, and then click a command and drag it to your new toolbar.**

   Drag the command right onto the toolbar.

6. **Optionally, insert divider lines between buttons.**

   Select the button to the right of where you want the line, click the Modify Selection button, and then choose Begin A Group.

7. **Click Close in the Customize dialog box.**

To remove a toolbar you've created, select its name in the Toolbars list on the Toolbars tab of the Customize dialog box, and click the Delete button. When Project asks if you're sure you want to delete this toolbar, click OK.

Customizing Menus

You customize menus in the same way that you customize toolbars, that is, by using the Customize dialog box. But before we get into the specifics, we need to take a look at personalized menus. In the Microsoft Office 2002 suite of products, of which Project is a part, the default setting is for menus to display the commands you most often use first and then display the full menu after a short delay. This feature pleases some users and annoys others. If you are among the latter, you can change this feature. To do so, take the following actions:

1. **Choose the Tools menu's Customize command, and then choose the submenu's Toolbars command.**

   Project displays the Customize dialog box.

2. **Click the Options tab.**

   Project displays the Options tab of the Customize dialog box, as shown in Figure C-8.

Figure C-8 The Options tab of the Customize dialog box.

3. **Clear the Show Full Menus After A Short Delay check box.**

   If you want to conserve screen real estate, clear the Show Standard And Formatting Toolbars On Two Rows check box. When you do so, Project combines these two toolbars. Obviously, there isn't enough room for all the buttons. To display those that are omitted, click the More Buttons button at the far right of the toolbar.

4. **Click Close.**

   To return your display to its original setting, click the Reset My Usage Data button on the Options tab of the Customize dialog box. Use the options in the Other section of this tab to display large icons, display font names in their font, and show or hide ScreenTips and their associated shortcut keys. If you want to animate menus, select an option from the Menu Animations drop-down list box.

Adding New Commands

As previously mentioned, you add commands to menus in much the same way that you add buttons to toolbars. To add a command to an existing menu, take the following actions:

1. **Choose the Tools menu's Customize command, and then choose the submenu's Toolbars command.**

   Project displays the Customize dialog box.

2 Click the Commands tab.

3. Select a category, and then click the title of the menu to which you want to add a command.

   Project opens the list of commands.

4. Click a command in the Commands list, and drag it to the location on the menu where you want it.

5. Click Close in the Customize dialog box.

Adding New Menus

Adding a new menu is similar to adding a new toolbar. To add a new menu, take the following actions:

1. Make sure that the menu bar is displayed on your screen.

2. Choose the Tools menu's Customize command, and then choose the submenu's Toolbars command.

   Project displays the Customize dialog box.

3. Click the Commands tab.

4. Scroll to the bottom of the Categories list, and select New Menu.

   New Menu now appears in the Commands list, as shown in Figure C-9.

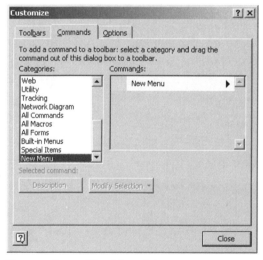

Figure C-9   The New Menu command now appears in the Commands list.

5. Click New Menu in the Commands list, and drag it up to the menu bar.

6. Click the Modify Selection button, and type a name for your new menu in the Name box.

   When you click the Modify Selection button, Project opens a menu of commands. Click outside the Modify Selection menu to close it.

7. Select a category, and then click a command and drag it to the menu.

   Drop it in the empty box that appears beneath your new menu.

8. Click Close in the Customize dialog box.

To remove a new menu you've added, open the Customize dialog box, click the new menu, drag it off the menu bar, and then click Close in the Customize dialog box.

Customizing a Table

You can also customize existing tables by inserting rows, deleting rows, changing the date format or the row height, and so on. And you can create new tables. We'll look first at how to make some changes to existing tables.

> **WARNING** *There is no Reset button in the More Tables dialog box, so make a copy of a table before editing it because your changes are permanent after you save the file. To make a copy of a table, in the More Tables dialog box, select the table name and then click the Copy button.*

Changing an Existing Table

You learned in "Step 3: Schedule Project Tasks" how to insert rows in a table, but you can also insert columns. Depending on the nature of your project, you may find that you need to track information that doesn't logically fit in any of the predefined columns. To add a column to the Entry table, take the following actions:

1. Open your project in Gantt Chart view.

2. Choose the View menu's Table command, and choose the submenu's More Tables command.

   Project displays the More Tables dialog box, as shown in Figure C-10.

Figure C-10 The More Tables dialog box.

3. **Select the name of the table you want to edit, and click the Copy button.**

   Project displays the Table Definition dialog box for that project. Figure C-11 shows the Table Definition dialog box for the book-publishing project.

Figure C-11 The Table Definition dialog box.

4. **Now you can do any of the following:**

   - Display the table's name in the More Tables dialog box by typing a new name in the Name box and selecting the Show In Menu check box.

   - Delete a row by selecting a field in the Field Name column, and clicking the Delete Row button.

   - Insert a row above the selected row by selecting a field, and clicking the Insert Row button.

- Change a column name by selecting it from the Field Name column and then selecting a new field name from the drop-down list.

- Change how the data are aligned in a column by selecting the column in the Align Data column and selecting Center, Right, or Left from the drop-down list.

- Change the width of a column by selecting it in the Width column and selecting a character width from the drop-down list.

- Change a title by selecting the column name in the Title column and typing a new name.

- Change how the title aligns by selecting it in the Align Title column and selecting Center, Right, or Left from the drop-down list.

- Change the date format by selecting an entry from the Date Format drop-down list box.

- Change the row height by using the Row Height spin box.

5. When you're finished making changes, click OK.

To insert a new column in a table, take the following actions:

1. Right-click the column head to the right of where you want to insert a new column.

2. Choose the shortcut menu's Insert Column command.

Project displays the Column Definition dialog box, as shown in Figure C-12.

Figure C-12 The Column Definition dialog box.

3. Select a field type for the column.

Select an entry from the Field Name drop-down list box.

4. Name the column.

Enter a name in the Title box.

5. **Specify how you want the title to align.**

   Select Center, Right, or Left from the Align Title drop-down list box.

6. **Specify how you want the data to align in the cells.**

   Select Center, Right, or Left from the Align Data drop-down list box.

7. **Rather than specify the character width, click the Best Fit button.**

8. **Click OK.**

Figure C-13 shows a new column, Summary, inserted in the project.

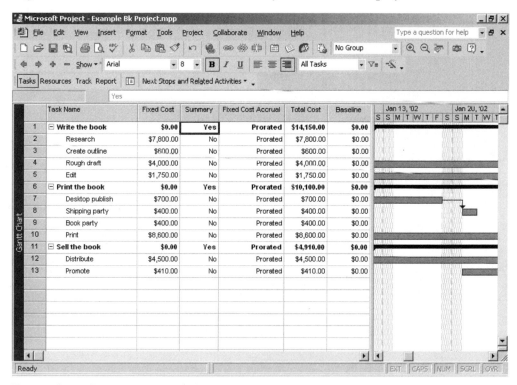

Figure C-13 Inserting a new column.

Creating a New Table

To create an entirely new table, take the following actions:

1. **Choose the View menu's Table command, and then choose the submenu's More Tables command.**

   Project displays the More Tables dialog box, as shown in Figure C-14.

Figure C-14 The More Tables dialog box.

2. Click the New button.

Project displays the Table Definition dialog box, as shown in Figure C-15.

Figure C-15 The Table Definition dialog box.

3. Name the table.

Enter a name in the Name box.

4. Specify a field name.

Click in the Field Name column, and select a field name from the drop-down list.

5. Specify the data alignment.

Click in the Align Data column, and select an alignment from the drop-down list.

6. **Click in the Width column, and accept the default character width.**

   You can adjust this width later by simply clicking between column titles.

7. **Click in the Title column, and enter a name for the column.**

8. **Specify the Title Alignment.**

   Click in the Align Title column, and select an alignment from the drop-down list.

9. **Repeat actions 4 through 9 to add more fields to your table.**

   TIP   *Use the Cut Row, Copy Row, Paste Row, Insert Row, and Delete Row buttons to facilitate field entry.*

10. **Specify the date format.**

    Accept the default date format, or select another from the Date Format drop-down list.

11. **Adjust the height of all rows.**

    Use the Row Height spin box to do this.

12. **If you want the first column of your table to remain on the screen when you scroll across, leave the Lock First Column check box selected.**

13. **When you're finished, click OK.**

    Back in the More Tables dialog box, click the Apply button to display your table on the screen.

Customizing the Gantt Chart

As you know from the steps in the first part of this book, you can change how the timescale is displayed in the Gantt chart by clicking on the Zoom In and Zoom Out buttons on the Standard toolbar, but you can also change the display of the Gantt chart in other ways. You can change the display of nonworking time, change the appearance of the bars, and add gridlines to a chart. We'll start with how to change the display of nonworking time.

TIP   *If you're the type who likes wizards, you may consider using the Gantt Chart Wizard to fashion a view to your liking. Click the Report button on the Project Guide toolbar and click the Change The Look Or Content Of The Gantt Chart hyperlink. You will be asked a bunch of questions about the Gantt chart you want, after which you will get your chart.*

Changing the Display of Nonworking Time

By default, the vertical bar that represents nonworking time is shown behind the task bars and thus the task bar appears to be running through nonworking days. If you find this confusing, you can change the display for nonworking time. Here are some other options:

- Display the nonworking time vertical bar in front of the task bar.
- Hide the nonworking time vertical bar.
- Display the nonworking time vertical bar in a different color and with a different pattern.

To change how Project displays nonworking time, take the following actions:

1. **In Gantt Chart view, double-click the vertical gray bar that represents nonworking time.**

    Project displays the Nonworking Time tab of the Timescale dialog box, as shown in Figure C-16.

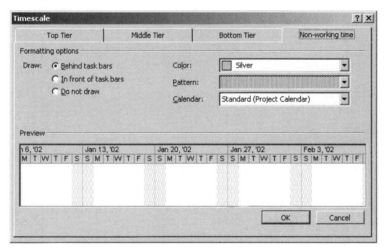

Figure C-16 The Nonworking Time tab of the Timescale dialog box.

2. **Click the In Front Of Task Bars option button.**

    Project displays the nonworking time bar in front of the task bars, as shown in Figure C-17.

Appendix C Customize Project   **245**

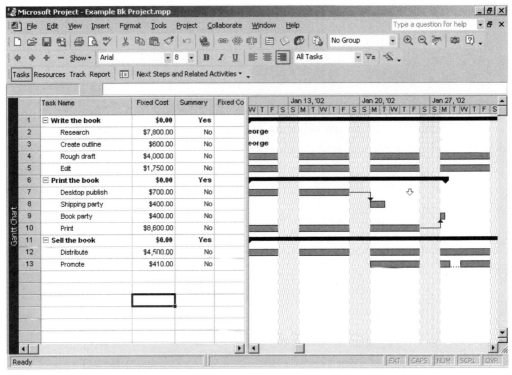

Figure C-17 Nonworking time displayed in front of the task bars.

3. **If you would rather not display nonworking time, click the Do Not Draw option button.**

   Figure C-18 shows how this looks.

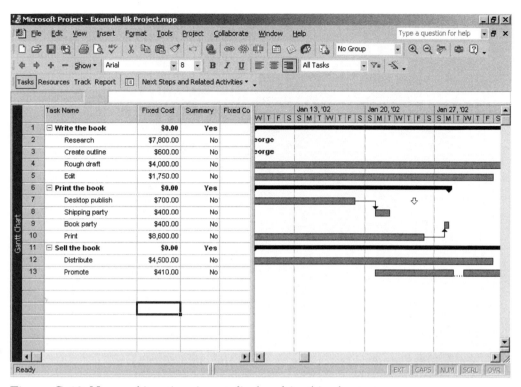

Figure C-18 Nonworking time is not displayed in this chart.

You can also choose to display the nonworking time bar in another color by selecting a color from the Color drop-down list. Change the pattern using the Pattern drop-down list.

4. When you're finished, click OK.

Changing the Appearance of Bars

To change the appearance of a single bar in the Gantt chart, take the following actions:

1. **Double-click the bar.**

   Project displays the Format Bar dialog box, as shown in Figure C-19.

Figure C-19 The Format Bar dialog box.

2. **Change the shape, pattern, type, and color of the bar.**

   To do this, use the options on the Bar Shape tab, as shown in Figure C-19.

3. **Click the Bar Text tab to change the position of text and to change the displayed text.**

   Figure C-20 shows this tab.

Figure C-20 The Bar Text tab of the Format Bar dialog box.

4. **When you're finished, click OK.**

   To return the bar to its original style, click the Reset button in the Format Bar dialog box.

Changing the Appearance of All Bars

To change the appearance of all bars in the Gantt chart, take the following actions:

1. **Double-click anywhere in the working area of the chart.**

   Project displays the Bar Styles dialog box, as shown in Figure C-21.

Figure C-21 The Bar Styles dialog box.

2. **Select an item in the Appearance column, and then make your changes in the bottom portion of the dialog box.**

   This area is similar to the Bar Shape tab of the Format Bar dialog box.

3. **When you're finished, click OK.**

Adding Gridlines to the Chart

Some users find it helpful to extend the lines that separate items in the Entry table all the way through the Gantt chart. To add these gridlines to your chart, take the following actions:

1. **Right-click anywhere in the Gantt chart, and choose the shortcut menu's Gridlines command.**

   Project displays the Gridlines dialog box, as shown in Figure C-22.

Figure C-22 The Gridlines dialog box.

2. Select Gantt Rows in the Line To Change list.

3. Select a line type in the Type drop-down list, and select a color for your gridlines in the Color drop-down list.

   If you want to spread your guidelines, select an interval. None displays gridlines spaced an item's width apart, 2 displays gridlines two item's widths apart, and so on.

4. When you're finished, click OK.

   Figure C-23 shows gridlines added to the chart in the book-publishing project.

Figure C-23 Gridlines added to the Gantt chart.

Changing the Default View

If you typically work in a view other than Gantt Chart view, you might want to make it easy on yourself and change the default view. To do so, take the following actions:

1. **Choose the Tools menu's Options command.**

    Project displays the Options dialog box, as shown in Figure C-24.

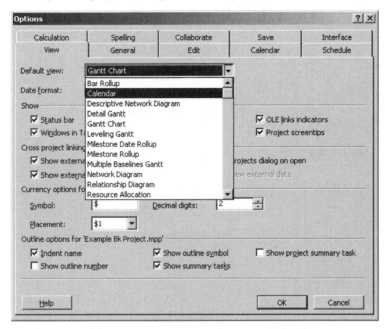

Figure C-24 The View tab of the Options dialog box.

2. **Select a view from the Default View drop-down list.**

    This is the view you will see every time you open a project.

3. **Click OK.**

GLOSSARY

Accrual method
The practice of recording costs for **resources** when the costs are incurred, which may be at the start of the **task**, at the finish of the task, or prorated.

ACWP
An abbreviation for Actual Cost of Work Performed. The actual cost of work already completed by a specific date.

AutoFilter
A **filter** that applies to a single column in a **Gantt chart**.

BAC
An abbreviation for Budgeted At Completion. This amount shows the total planned cost.

baseline
A snapshot of a **project** that shows all aspects of a project. You can use it to compare actual progress with planned progress.

BCWP
An abbreviation for Budgeted Cost of Work Performed. This amount shows the planned value of the work completed.

BCWS
An abbreviation for Budgeted Cost of Work Scheduled. This amount shows the planned value of the work originally scheduled.

chart
A graphical representation of **project** information.

Combination view
A split window that shows one **view** in the top pane and another view in the bottom pane.

constraint
A restriction that limits the start or finish of a **task**.

critical path
The series of **tasks** that must be completed on time in order for a **project** to finish on **schedule**.

critical task
A task on the **critical path**.

CV
An abbreviation for Cost Variance. This amount shows the difference between **BCWP** and **ACWP**.

deliverable
The outcome that must be produced to complete a **project** or a **task**.

dependency
A relationship between **tasks**. Because one task depends on another, it might need to start before or after the other task or at some point during work on the other task.

duration
The time it will take to complete a **task**. If a task will take one week to complete, for example, you can say its duration equals one week.

EAC
An abbreviation for Estimated At Completion. This amount shows the total actual cost incurred to date plus the remaining planned costs.

earned value

The value of work completed; the same as **BCWP**.

earned value analysis

The process of comparing the planned progress and cost of a **task** with the actual progress and cost.

export map

Instructions about what and in what format Microsoft Project information will be exported to another application.

filter

A Microsoft Project tool that you can use to display only certain information about a **project**, for example, only **tasks** that have been completed by a specified date.

fixed cost

A cost that does not increase or decrease over time, for example, a one-time licensing fee.

Gantt chart

A graphical representation of information in a **project**; named for Henry Gantt who in the nineteenth century introduced this method of displaying information in a bar chart/spreadsheet fashion.

GIF

An abbreviation for Graphics Interchange Format. A format originally developed for on-screen display that results in relatively small graphics files.

Highlighted Filter view

Displays **filtered** tasks or **resources** in a color different from that of the other **tasks** or resources.

HTML

An abbreviation for HyperText Markup Language; the language used to create documents that display in a web browser.

hyperlink

Text or a graphic in an **HTML** document that displays in a distinct manner (usually in a different color and underlined). Clicking a hyperlink takes you to another resource that can be on your computer, your **local area network** or **intranet,** or the **Internet.**

Internet

The world's largest computer network, connecting tens of millions of users.

intranet

A private corporate network that uses the **Internet** technology.

Isolated Filter view

Displays only the **filtered** tasks or **resources.**

lag time

The amount of down time between the end of one **task** and the start of another.

lead time

The amount of time that dependent **tasks** overlap. For example, if one task can start when the other is half finished, the lead time is 50 percent.

legend

The information at the bottom of a printed **chart** that explains the graphical elements used in the chart, such as lines and symbols.

leveling

Resolving **resource** conflicts. You can level resources manually, or you can let Microsoft Project do it automatically.

linking

Creating a **dependency** between **tasks.**

local area network

Abbreviated LAN. A group of computers and peripherals that are connected and that can share resources. A LAN usually connects computers within a single building.

milestone
A **task** that indicates the beginning or end of a task and that is a significant event in a **project.**

MPD
The file extension that saves an entire **project** file in database format.

MPP
The default project file extension.

MPT
The template file extension.

MPX
The file extension that saves a **project** file in ASCII, record-based text format so that it can be transferred between applications that support the MPX file format.

Network Diagram
A diagram in Project that tracks task flow. Also called **PERT** charts.

nonworking time
Weekends, holidays, or any other dates on which the people involved in a **project** do not work on the project.

overallocation
Assigning more **tasks** to a **resource** than the resource can accomplish in the time allotted.

outdent
Move a **task** to the left (and thus to a higher level) in the Task Name field so that it becomes a **summary task.**

PERT
A method for tracking **task** flow. PERT is an acronym for Program Evaluation and Review Technique and was developed in the 1950s by the Special Projects Office of the U.S. Navy. Project also calls **PERT** charts **Network Diagrams.**

PivotTable

A Microsoft Excel table that summarizes information into rows and columns that you can rotate.

predecessor

A **task** that must be accomplished before some other task, known as a **successor,** can be started.

project

A set of **tasks** that collectively achieve some objective. Typically, the tasks must be accomplished in a specified order and require **resources**.

Project Guide

The task pane that appears on the left side of the Project screen with instructions for completing tasks. The Project Guide toolbar offers buttons for switching from Project Guide to Project Guide.

project management

The art and science of organizing **tasks** in such a way as to control their progress.

report

A method for organizing and formatting **project** information so that it can be printed.

resource leveling

Rescheduling a project's **tasks** so that **resource** overallocations are eliminated.

resource pool

A group of **resources** that you can use to make **task** assignments.

resources

The workers and tools needed to accomplish a **task**.

schedule

The time and sequence of **tasks** in a **project**.

slack

The amount of time that a **task** can slip before it affects a **dependency** or the **project** completion date.

slippage

The delay of a **task** from its **baseline** plan.

sorting

Rearranging information in a **project** so that it is displayed in a different way. For example, you might sort **resources** in alphabetic order.

stakeholder

Any person who is involved or affected by a **project**.

subtask

A **task** that is subordinate to a **summary task**.

successor

A **task** that can be accomplished only after a **predecessor,** or prerequisite task, has been completed.

summary task

A **task** that is made up of subordinate tasks.

SV

An abbreviation for Schedule Variance. This amount shows the difference between the **BCWS** and the **BCWP**.

task

The basic building block of a **project,** a task constitutes a discrete amount of work often performed by a specific person at a specific time.

task ID

A number that Microsoft Project associates with each **task**.

template
A predefined pattern that you can use as the basis for setting up a **project**. To work with a template, choose the File menu's New command, and select a template from the lists on the Project Templates tab or the Office 97 Templates tab.

timescale
A graphical representation that appears at the top of a **chart** and shows a calendar in various **views** that you can define. By default, the timescale shows the weeks and days.

VAC
An abbreviation for Variance At Completion. This amount shows the difference between the **BAC** and the **EAC**.

view
One of the various ways to display information in Microsoft Project.

WBS
An abbreviation for Work Breakdown Structure. This **project-management** system organizes **tasks** to facilitate detailed **reporting** and tracking of costs. Microsoft Project uses the WBS outlining structure.

work
The total number of hours required to complete a **task**.

workgroup
A group of people who work on the same **project**.

INDEX

A

Access, importing Project information to, 163, 168
assigning resources, 60-61
assignment reports, 157-159
attachments to e-mail, 208
AutoFilter command, 107, 111-113

B

Bar Rollup view, 120
baselines, 21, 177-179
    changing, 179
    saving, using Track button, 178
    setting, 178-179
Budget report, 188
buttons on toolbars, add/delete/change, 230-234

C

Calendar view, 16-17, 30, 120, 122-125
calendars, 30-36
    Calendar view, 16-17, 30, 120, 122-125
    Change Working Time dialog for, 31
    copying existing schedule information to, 32, 70
    creating, 31, 69
    editing contents of, 71-74
    exceptions to workday/workweek in, 34-35, 73
    naming, 31-32, 70
    nonworking days in, 33, 34, 70, 72-73
    removing, 36
    in resource allocation, 69-74
    saving, 35, 70, 74
    seasonal or part-time work in, 73-74
    template and, adding a calendar to, 35-36
    wizard for, 30
    workweek and workday defined for, 32-33, 70
Cash Flow report, 187
Chart view, 119
collaboration options, 202-203
collapsing tasks, in outline, 97
communicating project status, 201-212
    assigning tasks/projects via e-mail in, 206-208
    collaboration options in, 202-203
    e-mail addresses for, 204-206
    e-mail collaboration in, 203-206
    Microsoft Project Server and, 202
    posting Project Files to public folders for, 212
    Project Central Service and, 202
    requesting progress information in, 209-210
    routing files to others for, 211-212
    sending Project Files via e-mail in, 210
    updating tasks assignments in, 209
communicating project status, 201-212
complexities in project management, 213-222
conflicts, in scheduling, 56-58
consolidated Project Files, for multiple projects, 223-225
constraints
    conflicting dependencies and, 56-58
    in scheduling, 53-58
    viewing, on Gantt chart, 56
Copy and Paste, to import Project information, 163
costing, 184-192
    Budget report for, 188
    Cash Flow report for, 187
    earned value analysis in, 197-200
    estimating, 185-186
    indirect, estimates of, 184

costing *continued*
    overhead, estimates of, 184
    recording actual costs in, 188-190
    reports for, 186-188, 191-192
    reviewing actual costs in, 191-192
    reviewing estimates of, 186-188
costs assigned to resources, 82-84
critical paths, 7-8
Critical Tasks report, 155
currency, 63
customizing Project 2002, 229-251
    Gantt charts, 244-251
    menus, 236-239
    tables, 239-244
    toolbars, 229-236

D

deadlines, 55-56
decimal places, 63
deleting summary tasks, in outline, 94-96
demoting tasks, in outline, 93-94
dependencies, 3, 4, 213-215
    conflicting constraints in, 56-58, 56
    Finish-to-Finish (FF), 53
    Finish-to-Start (FS), 52, 53
    lag time and, 213-215
    removing, 50
    in scheduling, 48-53
    setting type of, 53
    simplifying, 213-215
    Start-to-finish (SF), 53
    Start-to-start (SS), 53
    subtasks and, 214-215
describing a project. *See* Project Files, 23-38
Descriptive Network Diagram view, 120
Detail Gantt view, 120, 129
durations, 5-7, 39-47
    Effort Driven, 67
    estimating, 42
    fine tuning values for, 48
    fixed, 66
    fixed work, 66-67
    fixed-unit, 65
    in managing project progress, 184
    in resource allocation, fine tuning, 65-68
    resource leveling and, 78-82
    time lag between tasks and, 52

E

early finish date/time, 8-9
early start date/time, 8-9
earned value analysis, 12-13, 197-200
    amounts reported by, value and description, 198
    viewing report for, 199-200
    viewing tables of, 198-199
Earned Value report, 199-200
editing summary tasks, in outline, 94-96
Effort Driven duration, 67
e-mail collaboration on projects, 203-206
    addresses and address book for, 204-206
    assigning tasks/projects via, 206-208
    attachments in, 208
    posting Project Files to public folders for, 212
    requesting progress information via, 210-211
    routing files to others for, 211-212
    sending Project File via, 210
    updating assignments in, 209
equipment. *See* resource allocation and management
estimating costs, 185-186
estimating time required, 5
Excel, importing Project information to, 163, 164-167
expanding tasks, in outline, 97
export maps, 163, 170-172
Export Wizard, 163
exporting Project information, 163-176
    to Access, 163, 168
    Copy and Paste for, 163
    to Excel, 163, 164-167
    export maps for, 163, 170-172
    Export Wizard for, 163
    to graphics files, 163, 174-176
    to HTML or Web page, 163, 168-169
    to Word, 163, 172-174

F

File menu, Recently Used File List in, 27
Filter Box, 107, 110
Filtered For command, 107, 108-109
filters, 102-116
    accessing, 107, 108, 110
    AutoFilter command for, 107, 111-113
    creating your own, 114-116
    editing existing, 114-115
    Filter box for, 107, 110

Filtered For command and, 107, 108-109
highlighted view in, 109
interactive, 113-114
isolated view in, 108
More Filters command and, 107, 108, 110-111
resource, 103, 106-107
selecting, 107
standard, 103-113
task, 103, 104-105
tools for, 107
finish date/time, 8-9, 8
Finish-to-Finish (FF) dependencies, 53
Finish-to-Start (FS) dependencies, 52, 53
fixed duration, 66
fixed unit duration, 65
fixed unit tasks, 65
fixed-work durations, 66-67
flowcharts, 125
fonts, in reports, 160
footers for printed pages, 146-147
Form view, 119
Formatting toolbar, out/in outlining, 91-93

Gantt chart, 89, 121, 244-251
    appearance of bars in, changing, 248, 249
    AutoFilter command for, 111-113
    changing display of nonworking time in, 245-247
    constraints shown on, 56
    customizing, 244-251
    Default view of, changing, 251
    Detail Gantt view of, 120, 129
    Gantt Chart view of, 14-15, 118, 120
    gridlines in, 249-250
    Leveling Gantt view of, 120, 130
    Multiple Baseline Gantt view of, 120
    progress lines in, 195-197
    for resource allocation, 18
    in scheduling, 41-43
    timescale changes in, 100-102
    Tracking Gantt view for, 21, 121, 128, 192
    tracking/monitoring progress using, 21
    Wizard for, 244
    zooming in/out of, to view timescale, 100-102
Gantt Chart view, 14-15, 118, 120
goals, in scheduling, 53-58

graphics files, importing Project information to, 163, 174-176
gridlines, for Gantt chart, 249-250

headers in printed pages, 144-146
highlighted filter view, 109
HTML files, importing Project information to, 163, 168-169

I

indirect costs, 184
interactive filters, 113-114
isolated filter view, 108

keyboard shortcuts and macros, 219-222

lag time, 213-215
late finish date/time, 8-9
late start date/time, 8-9
legends for charts 147-148
Leveling Gantt view, 120, 130
leveling of resources, 11, 20, 78-82
    automatic method for, 79-82
    manual method for, 78-79
linking tasks, 3, 4, 49-50, 79
    multiple projects and, updating, 226

macros to automate actions, 219-222
managing project progress, 177-200
    baselines for, 177-179
    comparing progress with plan in, 192-197
    cost setting and updating in, 184-192
    durations in, 184
    earned value analysis in, 197-200
    progress lines in, 195-197
    start/finish dates in, 182-183
    Tracking Gantt view for, 192
    Tracking toolbar for, 180-181
    updating tasks in, 180-181
    updating the schedule in, 182-184
    Work tables for, 193-195

margin setting, for printing, 143-144
menus, 236-239
    adding new commands to, 237-238
    adding new, 238-239
Microsoft Project Server, 202
Milestone Date Rollup view, 120
Milestone Rollup view, 120
milestones, 5, 54-55
    Milestone Date Rollup view, 120
    Milestone Rollup view, 120
monitoring planned vs. realized outcomes, 2, 12-13, 21
More Filters command, 107, 108, 110-111
Multiple Baseline Gantt view, 120
multiple project management, 223-228
    consolidated Project Files for, 223-229
    linking source projects in, updating, 226
    linking tasks across separate Project Files for, 227-228

N

Network Diagrams. *See also* PERT analysis/PERT charts, 15-16, 125-126
nonworking days in calendar, 33, 34
nonworking time display, 245-247
numbering, in outline, 97-100

O

organizing project components, 2, 3-5, 14-16
orientation of paper (landscape vs. portrait), 142
outlining a project, 89-100
    collapsing and expanding tasks in, 97
    deleting summary tasks in, 94-96
    editing summary tasks in, 94-96
    Formatting toolbar and, 91-93
    moving tasks and summary tasks in, 96-97
    Planning Wizard and, 95
    promoting and demoting tasks in, 93-94
    summary tasks in, 90-91
    symbols and numbers added to, 97-100
    tools for, 91-93
    top up vs. bottom down methods for, 90-91
    Work Breakdown Structure (WBS) codes vs., 219
overallocation of resources, 11, 18-20, 80-81
overhead costs, 184
overlapping tasks, in scheduling, 51
Overview reports, 155

P

page breaks, in printing, 150
Page Setup, 141-149
paper size, in printing, 142-143
part-time resource allocation, 68, 73-74
password protected files, 25
paths, 5-6
paths, critical, 7-8
PERT analysis, PERT charts. *See also* Network Diagrams, 4, 15-16, 126
Planning Wizard, out/in outlining, 95
pool. *See* resource pool
posting Project Files to public folders, 212
predecessor tasks, 3, 49-50
presenting project to stakeholders, 137-176
    exporting Project information to other applications in, 163-176
    printing views of the project for, 138-150
    reports for, 151-163
Print Preview and toolbar, 138-141
printing, 138-150
    footers for pages in, 146-147
    headers for pages in, 144-146
    legends for charts in, 147-148
    margin setting for, 143-144
    orientation of paper for (landscape vs. portrait), 142
    page breaks in, 150
    Page Setup for, 141-149
    Page tab of Page Setup dialog, 142-143
    Print Dialog box for, 149-150
    Print Preview and toolbar for, 139-141
    reports and, 151-163
    scaling and paper size in, 142-143
    selecting what to print in, 150
    timescale selection for, 150
    View tab of Page Setup dialog for, 148-149
prioritizing tasks, 55-56, 79
Program Evaluation and Review Technique. *See* PERT analysis/PERT chart
progress lines, 195-197
Project Central Service, 202
Project Files, 23-38
    calendar setup for, 30-36
    creating, 23-25
    e-mailing, 210
    folders and directories for, 25-27
    linking tasks across, for multiple projects, 227-228

multiple open, windowed display of, 28
multiple projects and consolidation of, 223-229
naming, 24
opening, 27-28
posting Project Files to public folders for, 212
Project screen customization and organization for, 36-38
properties designated for, 28, 29
saving, 24, 25-27
shared resource pool and, 86
subproject divisions within, 215
templates for, 24
Project Guide task pane, 36-37
Project Information command, start/finish dates/times, 29-30
project management basics, 2
    monitoring planned vs. realized outcomes in, 2, 12-13, 21
    organizing and showing individual project components in, 2, 3-5, 14-16
    Project 2002 features for, 14-21
    resource allocation and management in, 2, 10-11, 18-20
    timing of tasks in, 2, 5-9, 16-17
Project screen customization and organization, 36-38
"project" defined, 2
promoting tasks, in outline, 93-94
Properties setting for files, 28, 29

R

read-only files, 25
Recently Used File List, for File menu, 27
recurring tasks, 43, 45-47
Relationship Diagram view, 120
relationships. *See* linking tasks
removing resources, 63-64
reports, 151-163
    Budget report for, 188
    Cash Flow report for, 187
    cost/in costing, 186-188, 191-192
    creating, from existing report, 161-163
    Critical Tasks, 155
    current activities and, 156-157
    customizing, 159-161
    Earned Value, 199-200
    font selection for, 160
    Overview Category of, 155
    predefined, by category and type, 151-153
    Print Previewing, 154
    Reports Dialog box for, 153-155
    selecting a predefined type of, 154
    Tasks Starting Soon, 156-157
    to-do lists and assignments in, 157-159
resource allocation and management, 2, 10-11, 18-20, 59-88
    assigning resources in, 60-61
    calendars for, creating, 69-71
    calendars for, editing, 71-74
    collapsing detail view of, 77
    costs assigned to resources in, 82-84
    currency setting in, 63
    duration calculations for, fine tuning, 65-68
    filters and, 103, 106-107
    Gantt chart for, 18
    leveling in, 11, 20, 78-82
    locating or filtering view of, 63, 64
    overallocations in, 11, 18-20, 80-81
    part-time, 68, 73-74
    parts and equipment as, 61-63
    pool for, 85-86
    reassigning in, 61
    removing resources in, 63-64
    Resource Allocation view for, 120
    Resource Form view for, 120, 131
    Resource Graph view for, 76, 118, 119, 120
    resource graphs in, 18-19
    Resource Name Form view for, 120, 132
    Resource Names column of Gantt chart for, 59
    Resource Sheet Form view for, 121
    resource sheet in, 19-20
    Resource Sheet view for, 75, 119
    Resource Usage view for, 77, 119, 121
    restructuring, 79
    reviewing, 74-77
    sharing, 84-85
    shortages in, 11
    sorting resources for, 116-118
    standard rate assignment for, 83
    substitutions in, 64-65
    viewing, 74-77, 119
    Work tables for, 193-195
Resource Allocation view, 120
Resource Form view, 120, 131
Resource Graph view, 76, 118, 119, 120
resource graphs, 18-19

Resource Name Form view, 120, 132
resource pool, 85-86
Resource Sheet Form view, 119, 121
resource sheet, 19-20
Resource Sheet view, 75 76, 119
Resource Usage view, 77, 119, 121
reviewing project organization, 89-136
    collapsing and expanding tasks in, 97
    editing and deleting summary tasks in, 94-96
    filters for, 102-116
    moving tasks and summary tasks in, 96-97
    outlining in, 89-100
    Planning Wizard and, 95
    promoting and demoting tasks in, 93-94
    sorting tasks and resources for, 116-118
    summary tasks in, 90-91
    timescale changes in, 100-102
    views for, 118-136
routing files to others, 211-212

S

scaling, in printing, 142
scheduling project tasks, 39-58
    additional information on tasks, Task Information dialog, 47
    conflicting dependency constraints and, 56-58
    constraints in, 53-58
    deadline constraint dates in, 55-56
    dependencies in, 48-53
    describing the project for, 40
    duration estimation in, 42
    fine tuning duration values in, 48
    Gantt chart for, 41-43
    goals in, 53-58
    identifying and scheduling tasks in, 40-43
    linking tasks in, 49-50
    milestones in, 54-55
    overlapping tasks in, 51
    prioritizing tasks in, 55-56
    recurring tasks and, 43, 45-47
    splitting tasks in, 52
    subtasks in, 43-45
    time lag between tasks in, 52
    to-do lists and durations in, 39-47
seasonal resource allocation, 68, 73-74
sharing resources, 84-85
Sheet view, 119
shortage, resource, 11
simplifying the deliverable, 138
splitting tasks, in scheduling, 52
standard filters, 103-113
start date/time, 8-9
Start-to-Finish (SF) dependencies, 53
Start-to-Start (SS) dependencies, 53
start/finish dates, 29-30
    in managing project progress, 182-183
    Project Information command for, 29-30
status of project. See communicating project status
subprojects, 215
    consolidated Project Files for, 223-229
substituting resources, 64-65
subtasks, 3-4, 43-45, 90-91, 214-215
successor tasks, 3, 49-50
summary tasks, 90-91
symbols, outline, 97-100

T

tables
    changing existing, 239-242
    copying before editing in, 239
    creating, 242-244
    customizing, 239-244
task filters, 103, 104-105
Task Details Form view, 121, 133
Task Entry view, 121
Task Form view, 121
task lists, 4
Task Name Form view, 121
Task Sheet view, 121
Task Usage view, 121, 127
tasks, 3
    collapsing and expanding tasks, in outline, 97
    deleting, in outline, 94-96
    dependencies in, 48-53
    duration errors, 47
    duration values, 48
    editing, in outline, 94-96
    fixed unit, 65
    fixed work, 66-67
    identifying and scheduling, 40-43
    linking, 49-50, 79
    moving, in outline, 96-97
    overlapping, 51
    Planning Wizard and, 95

prioritizing, 55-56, 79
promoting and demoting, in outline, 93-94
recurring, 43, 45-47
removing a dependency from, 50
sorting, 116-118
splitting, 52
sub-, 43-45, 90-91
summary, 90-91
time lag between, 52
Tracking toolbar for, 180-181
updating, 180-181
Tasks Starting Soon report, 156-157
templates, Project File
 calendar added to, 35-36
time lag, 52
time measurements, abbreviations, 42
timescale
 changing, 100-102
 printing selection from, 150
timing of tasks, 2, 5-9, 16-17
 Calendar view for, 16-17
 critical paths in, 7-8
 duration of tasks in, 5-7
 estimating time required in, 5
 milestones and, 5
 paths and, 5-6
 start and finish dates and times in, 8-9
to-do lists, 17, 39-47, 157-159
toolbars, customizing and organizing, 36-37, 229-236
 adding and deleting buttons on, 230-232
 button images on, changing, 232-234
 creating, 234-236
Track button, saving baselines using, 178
Tracking Gantt chart, 21, 121, 128, 192
Tracking toolbar, 180-181

uncertainties in project scheduling, 213-217
updating the schedule, 182-184

versional differences, Project 2000 vs. Project 2002, 1
View menu/View bar, 37, 38, 37, 122-128
views, 118-136
 combining, 134
 creating new, 135-136

More Views command for, 128-133
printing (*See* printing views), 138-150
types of, 119-122
View menu and View bar for, 122-128
Work Breakdown Structure (WBS) codes, 216-219

Web pages, importing Project information to, 163, 168-169
WGSETUP.EXE for e-mail collaborations, 203
Word, importing Project information to, 163, 172-174
Work Breakdown Structure (WBS) codes, 216-219
Work tables, 193-195
workday defined for calendar, 32-33
workweek defined for calendar, 32-33
Write Reservation files, 25

zooming in/out, to view timescale, 100-102

The manuscript for this book was prepared and submitted to Redmond Technology Press in electronic form. Text files were prepared using Microsoft Word 2000. Pages were composed using PageMaker 6.5 for Windows, with text in Frutiger and Caslon. Composed files were delivered to the printer as electronic prepress files.

Project Editor

Paula Thurman

Layout

Minh-Tam S. Le

Indexer

Joann Woy